The World

According to Jack

A Dog's-Eye View with Self-Help Advice for Other Dogs

Jack "K-9" Newport

Assisted by John and Ann Newport

With a Foreword by Dr. Steven Farmer
Author, *Power Animals* and *Animal Spirit Guides*

Transcendent
——Publishing——

The World According to Jack
By Jack "K-9" Newport

Assisted by John Newport and Ann Newport

Transcendent Publishing
PO Box 66202
St. Pete Beach, FL 33736
www.transcendentpublishing.com
(800) 232-5087

Transcendent
——Publishing——

First Edition 2018 Transcendent Publishing

Director of Photography: Amber Luanne Hollinger

Photographic Design Specialist: Adam Ditt

ISBN-13: 978-0-9993125-6-8

Library of Congress Control Number: 2017961770

Printed in the United States of America.

This book is dedicated to pets and pet owners
everywhere, as well as to the millions of pet store
operators, veterinarians, shelter staff and volunteers,
and others working to improve the treatment of
pets throughout the world and their quality of life.

A portion of sales proceeds will be donated to friends of
animal shelters, and other organizations working to provide
humane treatment and improved quality of life
for domestic animals.

CONTENTS

FOREWORD

As an author and the proud owner of a 75-pound Labrador "puppy" I love good books about dogs. As you are about to discover, *The World According to Jack* is a most informative and highly entertaining read.

By a stroke of serendipity, John and Ann Newport rescued Jack from the pound on or about the same day we adopted a cute little puppy, a male yellow lab, and named him Sampson. Six weeks old when he arrived, we went through all the usual experiences that you have with a little puppy that is new to the world. He had to learn where to go to the bathroom (outside), what toys are his (a rope) and which ones are not (such as shoes), and when he would eat (vociferously!). My wife Jesseca and our girls, Serena, 11 years old and Arianna, 9 years old at the time, naturally fell in love with him at first sight.

I've come to understand some of the ways he communicates what he wants and continue to learn more each day. Of course, heading expectantly toward the door with his ears on alert and looking back pleadingly to me, it doesn't take a professional animal communicator to interpret what he is trying to get across. A few months ago I proudly announced to Jesseca that he had actually lifted his leg in a typical male dog behavior to mark his scent and announce to the dog world in our community that there was a new kid on the block. We were thrilled just as if we had a baby that had taken his first steps! Well, except for the one time he mistook my leg for a fire hydrant, but hey, an honest mistake. And whether I'm gone twenty minutes or a week he greets me with unbridled, pure joy, his entire body wiggling in sync with his tail wagging. Such love!

Often I have wondered what it would be like to get inside his head, to smell, see, and hear the world in the way he does. Now having a dog for the first time in decades, when John Newport approached me about writing this foreword I jumped at the chance. He sent me a few chapters and I was instantly impressed with the humor and sensitivity in those pages. Of course, the named author is their little dog Jack Newport, assisted by John and his wife Ann, and throughout the book you'll find a "dog's eye" view of his life and particularly his relationship with his humans, John and Ann.

Jack even has provided five chapters that are for dog's eyes only, as he clearly states at the beginning of these chapters. (Okay, I confess I read through these and can only hope that this never gets around to Jack—please don't tell him). These are pointedly focused on "Training Your Parents," which gives other dogs tips on how to persuade mom and dad to give them extra treats and to even work their way into sleeping on the bed with them.

Speaking of which, I was telling Jesseca about Chapter 14 "Staking Your Claim in Bed." We don't allow Sampson to sleep with us as he's just too big, though my wife has on occasion hinted at doing so. Recently we were relaxing in bed one morning and Sampson put his front paws up on one side, not wanting to be left out. Jesseca patted the bed and called him to come up and for the first time since we've had him he jumped up on the bed and curled up next to Jesseca as if it were a given. I swear he must have read that chapter as he sure knew which one of us to work on!

Sprinkled in with Jack's commentary on various subjects, his dad and mom jump in to add their own editorial comments. You'll find some fascinating and helpful facts about dogs interspersed with Jack's brilliant and often humorous takes on life and his relationship with his humans and how he has trained them.

For instance, he expounds on how dog owners—or a dog's parents—are less likely to suffer from depression, tend to have lower blood pressure, triglyceride and cholesterol levels, and have elevated levels of serotonin and dopamine that produce a calming effect. He also reports that dog owners over 65 make 30 percent fewer visits to their doctors. Anyone who has owned and loved a dog will be nodding their heads in agreement.

So I invite you, the reader, to partake in this journey with Jack and his humans. You'll find it entertaining, insightful and heart-warming, and you'll no doubt have many laughs along the way. By the way, if you're browsing this book at a bookstore, flip over to Chapter 6 "Everyone Needs a Hobby" for a sampling of Jack's off-the-wall humor at its best. Happy reading!

-Dr. Steven Farmer

Dr. Steven Farmer is a world-renowned author, retired psycho-therapist, shamanic practitioner, spiritual teacher and public speaker who conducts workshops on spiritual healing and related topics across the country and throughout the world. His extensive list of publications includes Animal Spirit Guides and Pocket Guide to Spirit Animals (Hay House, Inc.). For further information on Dr. Farmer and his programs visit his website www.earthmagic.net.

THE WORLD ACCORDING TO JACK

INTRODUCTION

This is Jack's dad, John Newport. It's been an exciting adventure assisting Jack with this project and getting to know him as my alter ego.

I should start with a few words about how he came into our lives. I had always been a cat person, opting for low-maintenance pet ownership. My wife Ann, however, has had several dogs throughout her life and it was obvious that she deeply missed her most recent dog, Ginger. Ginger, a rescue dog, was a Golden Brown Aussie with the sweetest disposition you could imagine. Sadly, she passed away a few years back.

One evening Ann and I were out driving to a movie and we came across a distraught little dog running around our neighborhood without a collar. We posted a note on the community mail box, and by the time a frantic young woman came over to pick him up I had been smitten with the joys of having a "full-grown little doggie" around the house.

Early the following week we drove down to the pound to begin our search. After a frustrating morning checking out countless numbers of dogs, just as we were about to leave I spotted a little mixed Chihuahua named "Jack" in a cage hiding under a much larger dog. We took him out to the get-acquainted area and he enthusiastically kept jumping up and licking my beard. Maybe the beard made him think I was part dog! Anyhow, we instantly bonded and the rest is history.

How Jack and I came to write this book together is a story in and of itself. During our honeymoon period with Jack, he constantly had us in stitches with his crazy antics and we were both captivated by his extreme sensitivity and perceptiveness. One morning as we were laughing over his latest escapade I said – "Hey, someone should write a book about this guy!" Ann agreed and I encouraged her to take this on. She immediately replied "John, I believe YOU should write that book! You're always pounding out those "save the world" books and opinion pieces – I'd LOVE to see you write a fun book for a change!"

I was intrigued by her suggestion and called Jack into my office to mull this over. Not surprisingly his vanity won out, and he agreed to the project under one non-negotiable condition – HE would be the senior author and I would assume the role of his obedient assistant. To settle our dispute we grabbed one of his toys, had a tug-of-war and he won, as always. As by that time I was totally hooked on the project I readily acceded to his terms. By his own admission Jack is a manipulator par excellence – that guy definitely has a way of getting what he wants!

One thing's for sure, you can learn a helluva lot spending months on end sitting behind the keyboard with your dog, getting inside his head and heart. Ann even tells me I'm beginning to pick up some of his traits. Now that's taking it a bit too far! By the way, I need to excuse myself for a moment and wander out to the back yard to take a pee.

A word of warning. At Jack's insistence, several of the chapters begin with a prominent notice proclaiming "For Dogs Only"; in fact he limits access to one chapter to *small dogs only.* For readers who can tolerate these occasional restrictions, you have a most special treat in store.

In this opus Jack will give you a dog's-eye view of the world around him, with commentary ranging from the depressing environment of the pound where we initially met him to musings regarding his obsessions with food (much to his Vet's disdain) and lizards. There are five "For Dogs Only" chapters in which he offers his sage advice on "training your parents," coupled with advice to fellow canines on earning your keep and serving as a surrogate marriage counselor on call to resolve any domestic disputes, among other items. You'll find him to be a credible and engaging author, despite (or perhaps because of) his wacky off-beat humor and flights to fantasy, culminating in his egomania that takes over in the final chapter as he contemplates his future following release of this book.

Take it from me, if you're not a dog lover already you most definitely will be by the time you finish this book. I could go on and on, but I hear Ann calling me to take the clothes out of the dryer just outside my office. "Sure honey, I'll be happy to help you as long as you reward me with a healthy serving of treats!"

Happy reading!

ACKNOWLEDGEMENTS

Jack: Hi I'm Jack, senior author for this outstanding project that will undoubtedly set a new record for ongoing inclusion on the New York Times best sellers list. I wish to acknowledge both the two-legged and four-legged creatures who have graciously lent me their support, encouragement and assistance in completing this opus.

By far my deepest debt of gratitude is to my human parents and collaborators on this book, John and Ann Newport. In a rare moment of humility (wow, am I being candid) I must admit that I couldn't have done it without you! You two are such a wonderful couple and absolutely the greatest mom and dad any dog could ask for. Mom, you are such an ongoing support and source of nurturance, it never fails to amaze me how you manage to put up with me and my off-the-wall antics. And dad, you're the strong one whom I run to for protection when the thunderstorms and lightning are raging outside during the monsoon season. And of course, dad, I am deeply indebted to you for your tireless assistance in completing this project. Mark my words, under my tutelage you'll someday emerge as a renowned author in your own right.

I am also grateful for the skilled and compassionate veterinary care I've received from the staff at Pusch Ridge Pet Clinic, a truly awesome team that has worked together to keep me hale and healthy throughout what at times has been a rather challenging endeavor. I do wish, however, that my Vet, Dr. Poage, would lay off chiding me on my weight gain every time I see him.

I am also grateful for the enthusiastic support (and treats) I've received from my human extended family in California and Colorado. I especially appreciate the support and hugs I've received from my aunts Laura and Janice, my human cousin Amber, as well as from my uncle David, his wife Sandra and son David Jr., together with their pug Ruby. And let's not forget the support and kindness bestowed on me by my mom's sisters Barbara and Shirley.

🐾

Jack's dad: I wish to acknowledge the many friends and associates who have contributed to this project through their support and encouragement, as well as for the inspiration and assistance they have graciously provided.

My deepest debt of gratitude is to my loving wife Ann, whose heart-felt support and encouragement has been my guiding light throughout this entire project. In addition to her constant loving support I am especially grateful for her editorial skills and awesome photography, which were invaluable in producing the book you hold in your hands. (Jack's Interjection: I'll never understand why humans get so schmaltzy with this stuff.)

I especially appreciate the contributions of my friend, fellow author and mentor Dr. Steven Farmer, who over a decade ago encouraged me to "get a burr under my bonnet" to write my first book. In addition to writing the foreword he has served as my constant cheer-leader inspiring me onward throughout this entire project.

Both Jack and I are indebted to our (human) extended family for their support and inspiration in the various forms this has taken. I am especially grateful to my mother, Mrs. Loveda Newport, who took up writing as a hobby upon retiring from teaching and inspired myself and my two brothers, Jim and Jerry, to each become published authors with several books under our belts. Major thanks are also due to the California and Colorado members of our extended family highlighted by Jack for their enthusiastic support and interest throughout this endeavor.

In particular I wish to highlight the contributions to this project by our granddaughter Amber Luanne Hollinger. Beginning an extended visit with us at the mid-point in our endeavor, she graciously took on responsibility for the lion's share of photos throughout this book. Speaking of photography talent, special thanks are also due to Amber's friend Adam Ditt and to Royal Howard, who took the back cover photo.

Other friends and mentors lending their support are too numerous to fully acknowledge. Hats off to Allison Janse, editor of my first book "The Wellness-Recovery Connection." Allison, you are truly dedicated to your craft and I thank you for your diligent oversight on my first book, which has been immeasurably helpful in my effectively collaborating with my canine mentor in our collective effort on the current book. I am also indebted to my high school English teacher John Morris for the knowledge and inspiration he imparted to me and my fellow students. On a more personal level I especially wish to thank some very special friends, including Rick MacMahon, Dave Loder, Steve and Evelyn Denys, John Triandefels, Larry Schnebly – former anchor for KGUN Tucson – and Pima County Supervisor and fellow dog lover Ray Carroll.

And finally, both Jack and I owe a deep debt of gratitude to our publisher, Shanda Trofe, CEO and President of Transcendent Publishing, who tirelessly shepherded our project to fruition while providing gracious and invaluable support and inspiration along the way. Shanda, we've been truly blessed to have you as our publisher, we couldn't have done it without you!

CHAPTER ONE
Why I Wrote This Book

*"For me, this book represents the
culmination of a lifelong dream."*

Ever since I was a tiny runt, I have *dreamed* about reading a
book written by a real dog describing the world around him
from a well-honed canine perspective. So for me this book
represents the culmination of a lifelong dream. I must admit I am
rather perturbed, however, by my dad's stealing my thunder by
recounting from his perspective how we came to write this book. Just

goes to show you, you've really got to keep tabs on those senior assistant authors and keep them in line!

Anyhow, once my dad and I agreed to explore this project we combed the bookshelves in the Pet section of our local Barnes & Noble. While there were a number of books (mainly novels) narrated from a dog's perspective, none of these titles cited the dog itself as the author. WOW, we thought, here's our chance to really make history! As you will learn, nothing excites my dad and myself as much as the lure of a good challenge. The set of photos below, taken by my mom early on in this project, depict the evolution of my thought processes. The last photo says it all – in addition to the prospect of attaining worldwide acclaim for our achievement, I was intrigued by the prospect of *making a bundle off this project,* which would ensure me an unlimited supply of high quality treats for the rest of my life. And we haven't even mentioned the movie rights (Lassie, eat your heart out!)

"WOW – My Dad and I are writing a book about me."

"I wonder what great things we'll say about me…"

"Hey – I'm going to be FAMOUS!"

In addition to my overriding motive of greed (how's that for honesty) this project also struck a responsive chord with my altruistic side. This, in turn, triggered my staunch insistence that our book be sub-titled "A Dog's – Eye View *with Self-Help Advice for Other Dogs.*"

Think about it, we canines are a grossly marginalized species, especially given the fact that our estimated population of 70 million constitutes close to 20% of our nation's total domestic population (two-leggeds and four leggeds combined, excluding cats). Furthermore, consider all of the abusive references to our species that permeate our culture, for example – "They're treating me like a dog" (most recently attributed to our 44th president), "the world is going to the dogs," and "I wouldn't turn a dog out on a night like this!" Oh I could go on and on about the degrading cultural stereotypes that have been misapplied to our species since the beginning of time.

As these inequities began to sink in, I began to embrace this project with a sense of fervor. While our two-legged co-inhabitants have created a highly developed infrastructure to enable them to navigate life's problems and bolster their self-esteem via the burgeoning psychotherapy industry and legions of self-help books, videos and websites, we canines are essentially left to our own devices when it comes to attempting to survive and thrive in this increasingly complex world.

Hence many sections of my book are strictly *for dogs only* – no human trespassing allowed. These include my five chapters on "Training Your (Human) Parents" and my "Advice to Other Dogs" sections at the end of most other chapters. Indeed, as we canines are still a disenfranchised minority, I zealously expound on the proactive steps we must take to turn around this sorry state of affairs in my closing chapter titled "Grand Finale."

In closing, both our human readers and my fellow canines are definitely in for a treat in the pages ahead. And speaking of treats, if you really like this book I invite you to send a hearty portion of treats my way. Read on!

CHAPTER TWO
My Previous Life

*"My brothers and sisters and I
were all runts of the litter."*

If you're about to be adopted by new human parents, my best advice is KEEP THEM GUESSING! It just makes sense. When a human baby is put up for adoption great precautions are made to secure the anonymity of the former parents. That way everyone gets a whole new fresh start.

In my case, keeping my newly adopted parents guessing was a real piece of cake. I have very foggy recall of my life prior to adoption, due to a severe case of Post Traumatic Stress Disorder (PTSD for the technically inclined) arising from the termination of my idyllic first 5 years of life when I was abruptly whisked off to the pound against my will. I will share further details regarding this devastating experience in the following chapter.

I'm sure you are all familiar with the saying "runt of the litter." In my case my brothers and sisters and I were ALL runts of the litter as a result of coming into this world as part Chihuahua and part Jack Russell (or something else). I was, however, definitely the "clown of the litter." Some say that my real mom had sipped one or two many nips of Tequila by the time I got around to joining the rest of the litter at "dinner time." My lateness at the table, so to speak, may well have been a function of my genetic predisposition. As my current human parents will readily attest, I most definitely am not a morning person. Early on I flunked out of obedience school and was forced to keep in the good graces of my human parents by assuming the role of family clown.

As best as I can recall, during my formative years I enjoyed a very happy home life. I was well fed, had the run of the house and my human family gracefully tolerated and even encouraged my clownish antics. In this warm, supportive environment I was blessed with excellent role models of unconditional love and tolerance. I also acquired my share of "street smarts," particularly when it came to creatively hustling table scraps at dinnertime and otherwise excelling in the art of winning friends and influencing people through manipulation. (Fellow canines don't despair, I'll offer specific pointers for learning and fine-tuning these essential survival skills in the following chapters.)

Unfortunately my life in this blissful Garden of Eden came to an abrupt halt when one day, without warning, I was forced into a car and driven off to the Pima County Animal Shelter. Being of a sensitive Chihuahua nature, this hellish experience scared the living you-know-what out of me – driving home a full appreciation of the saying "this shouldn't happen to a dog!" Stay tuned for further details on this darkest chapter of my life – my life in the pound.

CHAPTER THREE
The Pound

"The final insult was the so-called neutering surgery."

I'm familiar with the human saying "all good things must come to an end." But Jeeze, talk about drawing the "Go to Jail" card and being thrown into the slammer without even passing through purgatory!

That was my introduction to the Pima County Animal Shelter. Imagine being locked in a cage in cramped quarters, combined with a monotonous diet of jail food – never knowing if or when you might ultimately be set free. Add to that the incessant barking and whimpering of over a thousand dogs who spend much of their time scared out of their wits, afraid for their very lives.

Let me return for a moment to my role as author of this book. In preparation for this chapter my dad and I spent hours researching the programs of the Pima County Animal Care Center (the official name for the shelter). As summarized below we were most impressed by what we learned.

The shelter serves a metropolitan area of just over 1 million people, and over 20,000 pets arrive at the shelter each year. On peak days as many as 200 pets are admitted. I was amazed to learn that the shelter staff and volunteers expend an extraordinary amount of effort to alert area residents of no-kill options for pets whose owners are no longer able to care for them. Closer to home, at the shelter itself they go overboard in finding good homes for animals housed there whenever possible. These efforts include:

- Active listings on their website highlighting pets available for adoption. Also, they waive the adoption fee several weeks throughout the year. In addition they waive the adoption fee for all pets in the "silver whiskers" club (dogs and cats age 5 and older), as well as for all animals who have been in the shelter for over 2 weeks.

- Adoption outreach to the community in partnership with Pet Smart, which houses animals available for adoption at 4 locations throughout the county.

- An on-line Lost and Found service to link strays up with their anxious human parents.

- And most impressive of all the shelter recruits and trains a large cadre of volunteers who collectively log over 50,000 hours of service annually. Among other things, these volunteers serve as on-site adoption hosts to help prospective adoptive parents sort through the over-whelming number of pets to choose from. Thankfully, my parents linked up with me through the patience and courtesy of a very dedicated adoption host. Volunteers skilled in public speaking also reach out to residents throughout the county to educate them concerning adoption opportunities and other programs offered by the shelter.

- A Foster Care Program – I was particularly impressed by this program in which volunteers serve as "foster parents" for animals who are too young for adoption, as well as pets recovering from illness or surgery.

For more information on the Pima County Animal shelter I invite you to visit their website by googling "Pima Animal Care Center."

I especially encourage you to visit their donations page and donate $5 or whatever to help support their worthwhile programs.

※※

Returning to my own experience at the shelter, despite our quarters' overall cleanliness the pervasive smell of death served as a harsh reminder of our mortality and the unspeakable fate that could befall us at any time. It was as if we were all on death row, hoping and praying that we'd be among the fortunate ones to be granted a reprieve. In this gruesome environment I rapidly adopted St. Francis of Assisi as my patron saint. (In my new home, my human parents placed a statuette of St. Francis on the ledge looking out over the front yard, where I love to lie and soak up the delicious Arizona sun.)

Like my dad I am a staunch believer in reincarnation. One thing's for sure, if I ever come back as a human I'll emerge as a flaming animal rights activist! Did you know that an estimated 3-4 million dogs and cats are euthanized (I hate that word) each year? My experience in the pound has instilled in me a profound sense of compassion for my less fortunate brothers and sisters, as well as for the dedicated staff and volunteers who care for us at thousands of shelters across the country.

Speaking of animal rights, I particularly decry the fate of the millions of pent-up chickens and overcrowded cattle in industrial farming complexes throughout America's heartland, anxiously awaiting their deaths to satisfy the insatiable appetites of human carnivores. (OK, my Dad just accused me of being a hypocrite, reminding me that my favorite meals include an abundant topping of shredded chicken. Anyhow – Long live the vegans!)

Back to the pound – I learned that even in our captivity there was some solace to be had, at least by some of my more fortunate fellow inmates. We all had cage-mates, my own was a towering dachshund whom I would crawl underneath in sheer fright of this horrific environment. My new dad likes to tell me of an incident he observed when he and my new mom-to-be were scouring the pound in search of a prospective new addition to their family. Walking through countless rows of cages, they came across two large dogs sharing a cage where the male was gleefully humping the female, totally oblivious to the constant parade of human onlookers. And here I was, sharing my cell with an overgrown male dachshund. Lady Chihuahuas of the world – where were you in my hour of need?

Speaking of which, the final insult was the so-called neutering surgery. Here they shave your belly, put you under and sterilize you. I mean – what about MY rights? I don't recall ever placing my pawprint on an informed consent form! Where was the ASPCA when I needed them? My new dad enjoys reminding me that when they took me to my new home the hair had not grown back on my underbelly –

and that my "manhood" was so starkly evident that I could have easily moonlighted as a mascot for Chippendales!

My rescue: On or about my tenth day in the slammer, a tired looking human couple accompanied by a volunteer approached the cage where I was cowering beneath my roommate. While they were about to abandon their search and call it a day, the guy evidently liked something about me and said "Hey, let's give this one a test drive!"

The volunteer took me out of the cage and the four of us proceeded to a small outdoor get-acquainted area. I was fascinated by the guy's beard – I guess I thought this meant that he was part dog. When he picked me up I jumped up and kept licking, licking and licking his beard. He must have liked this, as he told his partner "Hey, this one's a live one – let's take him home!" The rest is history. In less than half an hour I was signed out and carried out to a van by my new parents as they chauffeured me to my new home in Oro Valley.

🐾

Advice to other dogs: Take it from me, I hope you *never* end up in the pound like I did. However, if you ever do you must *immediately* acquire and constantly practice your own unique set of survival skills. Act as if your life depended on this because believe me, it does! While some impounded dogs become surly and look upon the constant parade of humans up and down the rows of cages as an intrusion, they are most sadly ill-informed. *You must look upon each and every human visitor as your potential rescuer, which indeed they are!*

Yes, it's all too easy to go stir-crazy and sink into a bottomless pit of despair in the midst of this depressing and death-ridden environment. I know. I lapsed into that groove many times myself, but fortunately was always able to snap myself out of it. At times like this, my best advice is to kneel down on your haunches and utter a prayer to St. Francis from the bottom of your heart.

NOW HEAR THIS! You must *always* exude an upbeat, warm and charming demeanor to each and every human visitor. Our human companions are right on at least one thing – the eyes are, indeed, the window to the soul.

Learn to talk with your eyes! Your human visitors will pick up on the love and enthusiasm your eyes project, and you will hopefully become one of the fortunate ones. And above all else, *don't blow it* when your prospective new parents invite you to visit with them in the get-acquainted area. Sure you're nervous – however you must channel your nervousness outward in the form of energy and enthusiasm. If your prospective new parents are at all perceptive (and they must be, after all they've chosen to visit with YOU) they'll be bowled over by your radiant warmth and energy, and in no time at all you'll be off to your new home.

PS: Several months after I was adopted, my folks were walking me at a neighborhood park where we encountered a dog training class led by a woman who also volunteers at the shelter. She immediately recognized me and exclaimed "Oh – Hi Jack"! Not wanting to risk being "high-jacked" (pun intended) back to the pound, I ferociously tugged at the leash signaling "let's get outta here!" My folks and I made a bee-line to the car and immediately headed back home!

CHAPTER FOUR
My New Home

"I was determined to be on good behavior regarding my toilet manners. In fact, I held everything in the first several days."

My new parents pulled into the garage of a single level home in a very nice neighborhood in Oro Valley and my new dad carried me in. To be honest, I had rather mixed feelings. Sure, I was elated to have finally been sprung from the pound, and my new mom and dad seemed like a nice loving couple. At the same time I was scared out of my wits big time! You have to understand, I was just beginning to recover from my uprooting from my original home when I was kidnapped and dropped off at the pound – and here I was confronted with another major adjustment. Yet as I began to calm down I observed that my nostrils were being treated to a smorgasbord of culinary delights, and I sensed a pervasive feeling of warmth permeating throughout the entire dwelling. Not too shabby, I thought, maybe these new digs will work out just fine.

I spent the first several days compulsively running and sniffing throughout the entire house, checking and re-checking every square inch. Of course the first stop was always the kitchen, a veritable treasure trove of that most precious of all commodities – FOOD! Later on my dad tipped me off that my new mom is part Italian, and that's there's no such thing as a bad Italian cook.

I rapidly felt comfortable enough to begin staking out the territory and laying claim to what was rightfully mine for the taking. The living room, which my parents hardly ever use as they prefer to hang out in the family room, contains a nice long couch that I immediately claimed as my own. Turns out that was a wise move, as when my mom began bringing home a new toy for me almost every day I knew I was going to need all that space and then some. I also laid claim to some prime real estate on the adjacent widow shelf overlooking the front yard. This comfortable niche contains a large statuette of a Buddha boy propped face up while lying on his elbows, together with a statuette of St. Francis, numerous miniature desert animals and an abundance of Native American artifacts. I felt right at home here and cajoled my mom to bring me some soft mats and towels to lie on while basking in the sun. My dad, with an obvious twinge of envy refers to this area as "Jack's beach."

Moving on to one of my least favorite topics – potty training. While my earlier family made sure that I was housebroken, the PTSD I experienced from my ordeal in the pound necessitated the need for a refresher course.

I just wish my new dad hadn't sat me down and told me about my immediate predecessor, Djembe, a black terrier pup my parents had taken in several months previously who turned out to be a "dog from hell!"

My dad, who is quite perceptive, admits in retrospect that his suspicion was aroused by the eagerness of the shelter volunteers in pawning that guy off. As soon as my folks brought him home he began running throughout the house non-stop and aggressively *demanding* their attention virtually every waking moment. While my current mom would come to his defense – "after all, he's just a puppy" – this guy wore out his welcome really fast! In fact before the week was out my mom led the charge in exorcizing that demonic presence from their home.

According to my dad, Djembe was an "in-your-face-dog" if there ever was one. He seemed to really get it off on flaunting his disobedience to their commands – this was especially true in the realm of potty training. Ever being the loving mother, my mom would take him for long walks in the back yard to get him to "do his thing." Alas, he would always seem to come up dry, so to speak. Then when he got back into the house, as soon as her back was turned he would run into the living room and *proudly* dump a huge pile of you-know-what on the carpet! Luckily for him, my parents must hang out with St. Francis as they arranged to place him in a no-kill shelter, where he was eventually placed.

After hearing my dad's warning about my immediate predecessor, I was determined to be on utmost good behavior regarding my toilet manners. In fact, I was so intimidated that I held *everything* in for the first several days. When I finally gave myself permission to relieve myself I went to the opposite extreme, and for the next several mornings my parents were greeted by yellow stains and brown stuff on the carpet. My dad held his nose as he cleaned up my mess and my mom remained her usual kind-hearted self. Within the next few days we got the routine down to a science. I'd station myself by the back door when nature called, and my dad would faithfully take me out for my morning constitutional. All in all we weathered our first week together as a family just fine.

🐾

Advice to other dogs: Above all else, DON'T immediately rush in and try to take charge. Sure you're nervous, but this is the one time you need to be on your very best behavior. Remember, you're a *guest* in your new parents' home and you don't want to blow it at the start. Best to stay calm, observe and take your cues from your new family concerning how you can best fit it. There'll be plenty of time later to negotiate your turf and begin the lifelong process of training your new parents (more on this later). But for now *you're* the one who needs to adhere to the ground rules.

If there are other pets in the household, just remember that *you're* the new kid on the block. While holding firm, quietly observe and take your cues from the current occupants. If another dog (or God forbid a cat) charges to attack you, let your new parents intercede and call them off. Let *them* lay down the law on your behalf, which takes you off the hook with your new house-mates. Above all, *don't* indulge yourself in a knee-jerk barking rant (which I admit I am prone to do) to "show them who's boss." That will most assuredly backfire and you'll be headed out the door in a New York minute with a one-way ticket back to the slammer!

CHAPTER FIVE
My First Trip to My New Vet

"By the way, I managed to stick my dad with the tab!"

When I left the pound I brought home something I'd much rather have left behind – a killer case of kennel cough. In addition to my habit of hacking when I get overly excited, which my parents tell me results from a Chihuahua size trachea trying to accommodate a Jack Russell body, I began having coughing fits almost as soon as we entered the door. (Fellow canines, note that I was smart enough to consciously suppress this until I arrived safe and sound at my new home.) Needless to say my mom and dad were quite concerned and they booked me to see a vet the very next morning.

Arriving at the vet's: First I must digress and explain why they gave me the red carpet treatment when we got to the office. The papers from the pound stated that my former owner named me Jack (my dad says that was probably short for Jack Russell). My dad thought that "Jack" was too plain for a dog with my outstanding virtues (good for you dad), and started calling me "Capt Jack." He explained that he borrowed that moniker from a high school classmate who logged in over 1 million nautical miles piloting a passenger boat R/T between Long Island's south shore and Fire Island over his career as a ferry boat captain. So when they booked my appointment I was registered as Capt Jack.

Sure enough when we arrived the next morning I was treated like royalty by a cadre of pleasant young ladies. They put me on the scales and I thrived on all the female attention lavished upon me before they took us back to the exam room. Little did I know that the weigh-in ritual would come back to haunt me as my nemesis.

Despite that grand reception, as I was already preoccupied with adjusting to my new home I was pretty nervous during my first visit to a brand new vet. I was so resigned that I even let the assistant take my temperature with a rectal thermometer.

When they tried that on my next visit, however, I stood my ground and intimidated the assistant with my ferocious growling.

After all, fellow canines, we've got to draw the line somewhere! My dad tried to calm me down, explaining that he undergoes a similar procedure – they call it a digital prostate exam, whatever that is – at his annual physicals. My take – if my dad is willing to subject himself to that kind of abuse in the doctor's office that's his choice. But as far as I'm concerned, no way Jose! Doesn't that assistant realize that she's subjecting me to an extreme affront to my dignity? Again, where is the ASPCA when I really need them?

Anyhow getting back to my first visit, my doc joined us in the exam room and he was *really cool!* Turns out he has a Chihuahua of his own and he began waxing on and on about what a "cute dog" I was. He even got down on the floor and touched noses with me. Now that's a vet after my own heart.

My parents complained that I wasn't peeing or depositing doggie droppings, and the assistant took me back to another room. When we returned she reported that not only did I pee all over her, I also managed to leave a sizable pile of brown stuff on the table. Strange – on subsequent visits I always look for her – I wonder whatever happened to her.

🐾

The doc confirmed the kennel cough diagnosis and recommended two over-the-counter medications. They also gave my folks a bag of flavored stuff to wrap around my meds to "disguise" them, and sold them a big bag of doggie treats. I told myself "Man, I'm really getting to like this place!" With that all done the ladies bade me a fond farewell and we headed back home. By the way, I managed to stick my dad with the tab!

CHAPTER SIX
Everyone Needs a Hobby:
Jack's Mega-Obsession With Food

*"I can sum up my all-consuming
passion in one word – FOOD!"*

A hobby can be defined as a subject or endeavor that we joyfully pursue with an all-consuming interest. We *all* need hobbies or creative pursuits to bring an added dimension of zest and purpose to our otherwise ordinary lives. Fortunately for me, my adopted family provides abundant role models concerning the passionate pursuit of a hobby or avocation.

My mom, who is a most sensitive and creative spirit, excels in at least two major hobbies – cooking and photography. She spends hours on end tracking down creative recipes and turning them on their heads with her innovative modifications. As my dad likes to brag, she puts her whole heart and soul into every meal she prepares. She makes every dinner an occasion for joyful celebration! And when we're hiking in the desert she'll take literally hundreds of photos of the beauty that lies hidden in her surroundings, capturing breath-taking sights we ordinary mortals would completely miss.

My dad is an avid writer and is happiest when he is pounding out an article or opinion piece on his PC or working on his latest book. He is also an avid loafer, spending hours on end soaking up the sun on our back yard patio. My uncle David back in southern California is an avid mountain biker and my dad's middle brother Jim, now living in Thailand with his wife Wassana, is a wannabe blues singer who will pull together a back-up band at the drop of a hat.

My family also boasts its share of canine hobbyists. My canine predecessor, my mom's dog Ginger, filled up their rec room with her bone collection, and my dad reports that when his younger brothers were growing up their shaggy mutt Jet would join them in backyard basketball games. Unfortunately this proved to be a rather short-lived hobby for Jet, as one day one of the brothers decided to toss him through the hoop in a misguided teenage prank. Is it any wonder that later that day he ran away? I say smart move Jet!

By now you're probably wondering what I do for a hobby. I can sum up my all-consuming passion in life in one word – FOOD! As my dad shakes his head in dismay, in my world *food trumps everything* – PERIOD! While I normally disdain cats, I've got to admit that "Garfield" is my all-time-favorite comic strip. Good old pot-bellied Garfield, he obviously shares my passion for food. And while his svelte human parent John Arbuckle bags a sympathy date with the vet's office receptionist about once a year, ol' Garfield is a steady number with the prettiest feline on the block. Goes to show you – there *is* justice in this world.

As I'll discuss in further detail later on, I most definitely am not a morning person. When the clock goes off and my parents hop out of bed, I'll linger on the comforter and would stay there for hours if I had my way. However, as soon as I hear my mom rattling out in the kitchen I'll bolt out there faster than a streak of lightening!

Throughout the day I can ignore my folks for hours – only to magically appear by their side with my tail wagging 90 miles per hour as soon as one of them begins munching on a snack. And while I love to play catch and tug-of-war with my dad over one of my toys, I'll make a mad dash for the kitchen as soon as I hear my mom working out there. Plain and simple, in my book food trumps everything!

As you may recall, the movie Ratatouille stars Remy, a runt of a rat who develops a passion for cooking and heads off to Paris to become a world renown chef. Well, me and that little guy have a lot in common! While his mission in life is to serve up the most delectable dishes to ever grace a human palate, my whole reason for being on this planet is to EAT THEM. Man, we would really make a great pair!

🐾

Advice to other dogs: Before we leave this topic I need to expound on the art and science of begging – especially for table scraps. One of my core beliefs in life is that creatively hustling for one's fix of food is indeed a most worthy endeavor.

Now if you are a novice, don't despair, you're talking with THE EXPERT on this subject. Remember, the EYES have it. Standing before your parent (or any human who is close to food) and bowling them over with the love radiating from your eyes is the surest way to guilt-trip them into sharing their food with you, and to keep on sharing, sharing and sharing to your little heart's content. Remember the one about the New Yorker who jumped into a taxi and asked the driver "How do I get to Carnegie Hall?" and the cabbie's response was "Practice, practice, practice!" Well that's it in a nutshell. Fine tune your begging skills through daily practice and take it from me, you will *never* go hungry.

And if all else fails, get down on your haunches and pray to St. Alexis of Rome, the patron saint of beggars. We all reach a point in life where we need all the help we can get, so go for it. And Bon Appetite!

CHAPTER SEVEN
Weight Watchers for Dogs

*"Thanks to my turncoat vet, my dad takes me
down the hall for a weigh-in every week."*

A s I mentioned in the previous chapter food is my all-consuming passion. Earlier in the book I also described the weigh-in ritual that began on my first visit to the vet's office.

Flash forward to early February. So here we are at the vet's office for the third time. After I weighed in at 12.5 pounds (compared with 7.75 pounds my first visit) the Doc is chiding my parents about "killing me with kindness" and he and my dad are comparing my current body shape with that of a torpedo or a burrito. Hey c'mon guys, you're affronting my dignity already! Yeah, I know my dad is a health nut and I gotta admit he's not doing bad for 74 by any means. Yet back off guys – you're messing with my passion in life – FOOD! After all, with everything going on in the mid-East and the whole planet going to hell in a hand-basket, who knows how long any of us will be around anyhow. So my philosophy – simply put - is live for the moment and EAT, EAT AND BE MERRY!

So now, thanks to my turncoat vet, my dad has instituted a new ritual where he takes me down the hall for my weigh-in at the end of each week. First he gets on and weighs himself, then he picks me up and subtracts his weight from the total second reading. I HATE it when he does that, I mean for crying out loud how does he manage to stay so trim – is there no justice in this world?

The aftermath of these weekly weigh-ins is predictable – my dad and mom sit down and agonize over my weight gain, and through the middle of the next week my between meal snacks are severely curtailed. By mid-week, however, I've managed to wear them down (see my future chapter on "The Power of Guilt"), then I'm weighed in again at week's end and my crash diet begins once again. Well, that's enough on that topic for one day.

OK, a new day of writing begins, and I am fit to be tied. Now I've seen it all! This morning I peeked at a front page article on my dad's desk describing a project just launched by the University of Arizona – a study titled "Dogs as Probiotics." My dad explained that probiotics are live bacteria and yeasts that are good for people's digestive health. Basically the study sets forth to determine whether the positive microbes in dog owners' guts increase over the time they are living with dogs, whose digestive systems generally contain an abundance of probiotics.

Being that ample evidence exists that we do indeed make people happier and in some ways even healthier, the researchers are seeking to determine whether there is a biological component behind this. Now they don't need a cockamanie study to prove this – *of course* the abundance of probiotics in our canine guts will have a positive impact of those humans whom we grace with our presence. *Which leads me to my point* – if the probiotics in our guts do indeed favorably impact the health of our humans, then it follows that the *larger the dog's gut, the greater positive impact on our human parents' health!*

In other words, when it comes to our canine tummies "the more the merrier"! So again, Dr Poage and my dad, BACK OFF about my weight gain! In the spirit of altruism I will unselfishly continue to sacrifice my former show-dog figure if it will make my human parents happier and healthier! By the way, pass the table scraps, please.

🐾

Unconvinced by my logic, my dad just shared with me a recent post featuring former Murphy Brown star Candice Bergen proclaiming she's fat and lives to eat, adding that she's put on 30 pounds over the past 15 years. Now that's my kind of gal! God forbid, if anything should happen to my parents I'm heading out to Malibu and asking her to adopt me. So lighten up guys, why quibble over my comparatively minor weight gain of 4 ½ pounds?

Despite my infallible logic (I would've made a great lawyer), my dad continues with the weekly weigh-ins. The good news is that something seems to be working, for the past 2 weeks I've held steady at 10 pounds, so my mom and dad are backing off on the parentally imposed table scrap restrictions.

🐾

Advice to other dogs: Unless you suffer from a perverse aspiration to be a show dog, I urge you to follow my philosophy of "eat, eat and be merry!" If your parents are compulsive health-nuts like mine are, this will require heavy doses of *persistence* on your part. The key, of course, is *manipulation by guilt.* Remember – the eyes have it! So if they're trying to curtail your access to table scraps, persist in bounding up to them with your tail wagging non-stop. Then when they refuse to comply, shift gears and stare them down with your oh-so-sad guilt provoking eyes. Keep on persevering and trust me, you'll eventually wear them down!

CHAPTER EIGHT
Earning Your Keep

"Dale Carnegie stated over 50 years ago that a dog is the only creature that doesn't have to work for a living."

This chapter is directed to my canine brothers and sisters. Human readers can take a peak if you'd like – but this is absolutely *forbidden reading* for cats and mean large dogs!

My dad tells me that Dale Carnegie, author of "How to Win Friends and Influence People" stated well over 50 years ago that a dog is the only creature in the world that doesn't need to work for a living. He explained that we enjoy this privileged status as through the eons we have learned, possibly as a survival strategy, to generously lavish unconditional love on our human companions. Can you image an ox or a horse surrounding his or her owner with unconditional love? And guess what, they *work* for a living!

Some readers may argue that cats also enjoy this privileged status on account of the unconditional love and comforting they give their owners. From what I've observed, however, I submit that our feline cousins are grossly spoiled brats who have learned to con their way through life. My dad reminds me that I may be just a wee bit biased here. While of course I am – I'm a DOG and PROUD of it! And besides, would anyone in their right mind really want a pet that whiles away their days eating and sleeping? Regarding the last sentence, my dad simply shrugs his shoulders and says "no comment."

Now comes the good part where I share with you, my fellow canines, how to maintain your privileged status by keeping in good graces with your adopted family.

First of all – shower them with enthusiasm! Always be the first one out of bed (do as I say here, *not* as I do) and greet each and every family member with unbridled enthusiasm as they crawl out of bed. When I finally get up each morning I scamper around the house like a race horse, jump up on my hind legs and dance with both my mom and dad as they greet the day. OK, I also go right back to bed as soon as I've had my breakfast – I never claimed to be a morning person. Anyhow, the underlying psychology is perfect – if you help your family members get their day off to a cheerful start they'll be eternally grateful!

Along these same lines – keep them laughing! Everyone loves a clown, so ham it up to your heart's content. Be spontaneous – when your dad touches noses with you surprise him with a big lick on his nose, and invent all kinds of crazy games to keep them laughing with *you* as the center of attention. Several times a day my parents and I play a game of catch where they toss one of my many toys back and forth. Finally my dad whirls the toy around and tosses it into the other room for me to fetch. When I retrieve the toy we have a tug-of-war, and guess who always wins? (Yours truly)

I've saved the most important tip for last. Be constantly attentive, learn to *tune in* to each family member, and always be the first to comfort someone when they are down in the dumps. Sometimes my mom gets sad because she misses her family in California. And guess who immediately jumps up on her lap, looks at her with his big loving eyes, and keeps licking, licking and licking her face? And it works – as my mom tells both me and my dad, it's impossible to laugh and cry at the same time! And when my dad is down in the dumps, I'll just quietly lie down by his desk chair, letting him know I'm there for him.

So there you have it – Jack's 3-step program for eternally remaining in your human family's good graces.

🐾

If, however, you choose to work for a living there's a world of opportunity out there. If you have a flair for modeling and can endure the boredom of judging ceremonies, become a show dog. Some of the more noble occupations for working dogs include serving in the US Army K-9 Corps, Police Dogs, Fire House Dogs, Sheep Dogs and Service Dogs.

The Army launched its K-9 Corps during World War II, training thousands of dogs to guard facilities, carry messages, snuff out mines and pull sleds. Police dogs are specially trained to assist police in searching for drugs and explosives, as well as for lost people, helping to scope out evidence at the scene of a crime, and protecting their handlers. A word of caution – if you aspire to be a pot-sniffing police dog, be advised that most police departments will not reward you with a share of the cache (as of this writing, Alaska, California, Colorado, the District of Columbia, Oregon and Washington may be exceptions).

Fire house dogs have an interesting history, with Dalmatians serving as fire fighters' house mascots for generations. During the days of horse-drawn fire carriages they were used to shoo pedestrians off the road while the firemen were racing to the scene. They were also used to comfort both horses and firefighters and guard the fire-wagon. Throughout recorded history sheep dogs, particularly Australian Shepherds and other wolf-like dogs, have been used to herd and protect their flocks.

At the bottom of the barrel of working class dogs are the "mean old junk-yard dogs." I mean, what self-respecting canine would want to be kept at a state of virtual starvation to make them mean, while staying up all night guarding a junk-yard, closed gas station or whatever while everybody else is out partying!

Use of therapy dogs has proliferated over the past several decades. Legend has it that this tradition was started during World War II by "Smoky," a female Yorkshire Terrier abandoned on the battlefield who was rescued by an American corporal. Wounded soldiers at the base hospital welcomed her visits which cheered them up immensely, and Smoky's service as a therapy dog lasted 12 years both during and after World War II. Today therapy dogs trained to provide comfort to people in distress are used in hospitals, retirement homes, nursing homes, schools, hospices, on-site at disaster areas and as an aid to people suffering from autism and learning disorders.

My dad relates to me an incident involving use of their Australian Shepherd as a therapy dog to comfort a neighbor in distress – I'll let him share this with you in his own words.

Jack's Dad: Thanks Jack. Back when we were living in Santa Ana, California we had an older Aussie named Ginger whom Ann had rescued from the pound. Our next-door neighbor Wes was a gentleman well into his 90s who had outlived three wives. While he suffered from dementia during his later years, he was able to remain relatively independent as his family arranged for a housekeeper to care for him during the week. One Saturday afternoon as I was returning from my walk, Wes had left the house and was wandering on the sidewalk appearing rather confused and distraught. I intuited that Ginger's gentle disposition would comfort him and asked Ann to bring her over. Ginger came up and started licking the palms of his hands, and before we knew it he was sitting in the yard petting her and playing with her collar. We were then able to help him back into his house and Ann called his family for assistance.

Back to Jack: OK, back to the senior author. Many folks have commented that I would make an ideal therapy dog. While that may be true, I'll take a pass. I already have my hands full taking care of my own mom and dad (my dad, like most people with a PhD in psychology, is as nutty as they come), and providing marital therapy to boot! (See Chapter 17 for further details.)

One of the noblest callings embraced by canines is assisting people with disabilities as service dogs. In addition to dogs trained to guide the blind and visually impaired, there are also service dogs trained to alert people who are deaf, alert and protect a person having a seizure, remind a person with mental illness to take their medication, calm people with PTSD during anxiety attacks and perform other duties. I firmly believe that we gifted canines have a

corner on the market for service animals. C'mon, let's get serious –
can you imagine a "seeing eye cat" or a fire-fighting tom-cat?

Having provided a highlighting of some of the magnificent
qualities of our species that make us uniquely qualified to serve our
two-legged bothers and sisters in a healing capacity, we will expound
on this theme in the following chapter.

CHAPTER NINE
"Is Your Pet a Healer?"

*"Dogs have a profound healing impact on humans by
virtue of the unconditional love
they instinctively convey."*

The answer to the above question is a resounding YES, unless your pet happens to be one of those (fortunately rare) mean old junk-yard dogs!

Following completion of the preceding chapter, my dad and I agreed to more thoroughly research the healing connection between pets and their human parents. We were amazed at the plethora of research documenting this fascinating phenomenon.

Dr. Allen McConnell, a psychology professor at Miami University states: "Owning a pet gives you a sense of purpose and belonging that can increase feelings of positivity and lower stress levels, all of which translate to health benefits." He goes on to state that "Establishing an emotional bond with your pet, as you would a family member or friend, also pays a health bonus. *It's actually better for you to think of your animal as a furry person.*"

Wow, the good doctor said a mouthful there, a man after my own heart. I especially like his allusion to us as "furry people." Our canine species has, indeed, been marginalized far too long. Given that we comprise a whopping 20 percent of the nation's total population, two-leggeds and four-leggeds combined (excluding cats), it's high time we be awarded the status as full-fledged citizens we so richly deserve! I'll expound on this in the final chapter.

Returning to the theme of this chapter, Prevention magazine cites evidence that having a pet can decrease levels of cortisol, a stress hormone that can wreak havoc on the body, while raising levels of the feel good brain chemical dopamine. Research also shows that people with positive interactions with animals experience a boost in oxytocin, the hormone that promotes love and trust and is linked to reduced blood pressure and heart rate.

A New York Times piece documents the amazing ability we canines possess to detect serious health problems in people long before the person and his or her physician is aware of them. They report on a 2003 University of Florida study that noted that some dogs appear to have an innate ability to detect impending seizures. Likewise in 2006 the Journal of Integrated Cancer Therapies reported that some dogs have the ability to identify breast and lung cancer in patients by smelling their breath. And at the time the Times article went to press a University of Maine study was exploring whether dogs can sniff out ovarian cancer.

My dad, fluffing up his aura as a psychologist, reports he has observed some differences in healing interactions with humans on the part of dogs and cats, adding that his observations concerning my feline cousins are backed up by numerous literature references. Cats, he contends, often impart their healing energy to humans by absorbing excessive stress when people stroke them. Quoting him, "Back when I was working in the medical field I'd come home and spend several minutes stroking our Siamese cat Cooney. While Cooney was always very patient, when I'd stop petting him he would immediately 'shake it off', as if he were telling me 'Hey man, I want nothing to do with your accumulated stress!'" I would add that I respond similarly when my dad strokes me in the middle of a stressful day, though I'll admit I thoroughly enjoy his back rubs.

Dogs, he contends, tend to have a profound calming and healing impact on humans by virtue of the unconditional love, warmth and genuine caring they instinctively convey to people, unless they pick up warning signs that someone might pose a threat to them. To be sure there are exceptions, which my dad speculates are most likely to occur with a dog who was not raised in a caring home environment.

I asked my dad to expound on his thoughts concerning the unique healing bond that so often exists between pets and their human owners, and here's what he has to say.

Jack's Dad: I have always been impressed by what appears to be a mutually symbiotic bond of caring and healing that so often exists between pets and their humans. Domesticated animals, such as dogs and cats, have historically been conditioned to feel helpless without the benevolent grace their humans bestow upon them by caring for them. (Jack to his canine readers: OK, I'll let him have his say here, but rest assured I'll tear that myth apart in my forthcoming chapters on "Training Your Human Parents.")

Back to Jack's Dad: Being that pets tend to feel helpless without a loving human to care for them, they quite naturally feel beholden to their human parents. This sense of gratitude may in part explain why many, if not most, pets are inclined to want to look out for their humans and return the favor, so to speak.

Jack's immediate predecessor Ginger, a very warm-hearted Aussie, was totally devoted to Ann, who rescued her from the pound. Throughout her years with us she was an inseparable shadow to her human mom. And whenever Ann was feeling down, she would immediately run to her side to comfort her. With Jack there exists an incredible bond of healing and caring between him and both Ann and myself. He *knows* he is an integral part of our family; when Ann and I hug he will immediately run over to make it a three-way group hug. He is incredibly tuned into Ann's emotions, and always showers her with his full support whenever she is experiencing either physical or emotional discomfort.

I also recall decades ago witnessing a real bonding between my parents and their pets during their later years. Can you imagine bonding with a school of goldfish? As my dad was the one who fed them, they would excitedly jump up and down in the water whenever he walked past their fishbowl. A decade later when my mom lived alone with her soft and fluffy cat Whitey, they would spend the bulk of the day comforting each other with Whitey in my mom's lap as she watched television or read.

Back to Jack: Well dad, as they say in group therapy "Thanks for sharing that!" Now getting back to *my* readers, I'm sure you won't be the least surprised to learn that in wrapping up this discourse I've most definitely saved the best for last.

In completing my own (ahem) extensive component of this research, I came across a fascinating series of posts by Dr. Marty Becker, who bills himself as "America's Veterinarian." In addition to maintaining a dynamic interactive on line newsletter, this amazing guy has served as author, co-author or editor of 22 books about pets that together have sold more than 7 million copies, including three New York Times best-sellers. I would highly recommend his classic tome "The Healing Power of Pets," together with the numerous books on dogs, cats and other pets he has contributed to the "Chicken Soup for the Soul" series.

I was particularly intrigued by his recent series of posts on the "Healing Power of Pets." Quoting from one of these posts he states: "There are three things I am certain about pets.

- They would rather be with us in the streets than without us in a mansion

- Their very presence can make our lives better, richer, less stressful, and healthier

- They do more for us than we do for them, but they act like it's the other way around."

- A sampling of readers' comments expounding on this theme includes:

    o They can teach a person how to love again

    o If I could love even half as well as they, this world would be so much better

    o They remind us every day that true unconditional loves still exists in this otherwise harsh world.

🐾🐾

By far the most fascinating item by Dr. Becker I reviewed was a post concerning "diabetic alert dogs." He relates a true story involving Emily, a young woman who was diagnosed with Type 1 Diabetes at age 7. She battled blood sugar swings until she went off to college, when she discovered she could no longer tell when her blood sugar was dropping dangerously low, an incident that can cause coma or even death.

Fortunately, an organization called Early Alert Canines linked her up with a service dog named Fleur. Amazingly, Fleur had been trained to monitor subtle signs relating to Emily's blood sugar level and alert her when it is dropping toward the danger level. Quoting from Emily: "Every time she alerts me, I am amazed…I have no idea how many times Fleur has saved my life and kept me out of danger…I wish that every diabetic had the option of being placed with a diabetes alert dog."

To learn more about this amazing organization that trains dogs to serve as diabetic alert dogs, google www.EarlyAlertCanines.org. They are definitely performing a much needed life-saving service, and would gratefully welcome donations from interested readers.

This concludes my chapter on the healing power of members of our illustrious species. Building upon this expansive treatment of the bonding between pets and their humans, in the next chapter we will provide an exciting discourse concerning why dogs (and other animals) are psychic. Stay tuned.

CHAPTER TEN

Why Dogs and Other Animals are Psychic

Jack's Dad: "By far the greatest benefit we derive from our pets and other animals is that they teach us how to love."

L argely at my dad's insistence, we decided to research the subject of psychic phenomena in regard to animals and devote a chapter to that fascinating topic. As my dad took the lead on this one I'll let him begin.

Jack's Dad: Thanks Jack. Ever since my 30s I've been quite interested in psychic phenomena and as a pet owner (sorry, human parent) I've always thought that animals were highly versed in psychic communication. To me this makes a world of sense. As animal thought processes appear to be primarily visual and auditory (although some studies suggest that many pets understand a great many human words), it just makes sense that psychic exchanges might well play an important role in their communication with each other. I should clarify that to me the "psychic powers," which I believe we all possess to one degree or another, essentially flow from a highly developed sense of intuition, combined with a strong sense of empathy, or the ability to compassionately put oneself in another's shoes, so to speak.

An interesting article in New Renaissance Magazine titled "The Unexplained Powers of Animals" states that for many years animal trainers and pet owners (sic) have observed a heightened perceptiveness in animals that suggests the existence of psychic powers. The article also refers to household surveys conducted in both the USA and Britain in which close to 50 percent of all dog owners reported that their pets responded to their thoughts or silent commands. If domestic animals are telepathic with their humans, the article suggests it seems that animals are likewise telepathic with each other, and this may play an important role in animal behavior in the wild.

The authors also suggest that psychic or highly intuitive perception and communication appears to be more fully developed in animals than in humans. Among humans, they suggest that these powers seem to be better developed in indigenous cultures than in modern industrial society. Having spent a fair portion of my life in areas close to Native American communities, I have always been fascinated by the prominent role of communication with animal spirits in tribal traditions and legends passed down over many generations. Much of this stems, I believe, from the admirable respect these first Americans had for our earth mother and the wide variety of species walking the planet, knowing that we two-leggeds are just one of these many species.

And speaking of the highly developed psychic qualities of creatures in the wild, I have always been fascinated by the flight patterns of large flocks of birds as they perform intricate gyrations in the air, highly orchestrated movements in unison that mimic the skillfully coordinated formations of military jets on display at air shows. My own take here is that a flock of birds in flight manifests a highly orchestrated psychic connection, whereby the whole flock assumes the characteristics of one intricately coordinated mind.

Jack: Hey dad, so far what you're saying makes a great deal of sense. Please continue.

Jack's Dad: One of the articles we researched quotes an animal psychic as stating that dogs tends to be particularly psychic in regard to their human, in contrast to most other pets, as the dog often feels responsible for it's humans' well-being. They take their protector role very seriously. Dr. Rupert Sheldrake, a faculty member at England's Cambridge University, has extensively researched accounts pertaining to paranormal perceptions among animals. His data base of 5,000 case histories includes 177 accounts of dogs appearing to respond to the death of their *absent* masters or mistresses, mostly by howling, whining or whimpering.

Sheldrake also claims that animals appear to have a heightened sense of impending doom, which he contends cannot be readily explained by known physical phenomena. Describing a particularly impressive recounting of the phenomena he states: "According to villagers in Bang Koey, Thailand, a herd of buffalo were grazing by the beach when they suddenly lifted their heads and looked out to sea, ears standing upright. They turned and stampeded up the hill, followed by bewildered villagers, whose lives were saved from a major tsunami." He also claims that during World War II, many families relied on pets' behavior to warn of impending air raids when the enemy planes were still hundreds of miles away.

Anyhow, I'd like to shift gears a bit and talk about some episodes of psychic communication I've experienced with you and our other pets over the years.

Jack: Go for it – Dad!

Jack's Dad: Back when we first came to Arizona your mom and I brought down from Washington our elderly Siamese cat, Cooney, who had been our companion for many years. I tell you, buddy, that cat had an incredible sense of time and was a "walking alarm clock." Depending on the weather, I'd set my clock for sometime between 5:15 and 6:00 am to get up for my morning walk. This proved to be totally unnecessary, however, as every morning Cooney would come in to wake me just before my alarm went off!

What really blew my mind, however, was the morning I had set my clock for 4 am to catch my plane for a consulting gig back East. Unfortunately, I forgot to turn the alarm on. Not to worry, Cooney magically appeared and woke me up right at 4 am!

Jack: Man, that cat sounds scary – especially to me as I'm definitely not a morning person!

Jack's Dad: And speaking of cats, when we lived in the Northwest we also had a black and white tom-cat named Mystery. We rented out the cottage adjacent to our house to a Scrimshaw artist named Peter. Mystery would visit every morning, perched on top of the outside wall and peering down at him at his drawing table. One morning Peter said "Mystery, you're getting bored. You need to go out and catch a rat!" Here's the punch line – When Peter opened his front door the next morning he was greeted by a big old dead rat that Mystery obviously had left there!

Jack: Wow, sounds like two crazy cats!

Jack's Dad: Now I'd like to share with our readers some observations concerning the telepathic communication that both your mom and I have experienced with you. I've always been impressed that you are particularly tuned in to Ann's feelings, especially when she is experiencing any form of stress or discomfort. You are immediately right there with her, lying on her belly and comforting her immensely with your loving presence. You are truly man's – and woman's – best friend.

Having said that, buddy, I also need to let our readers know that you mischievously use your psychic abilities to the hilt in man-ipulating me and your mom into caving in to your demands. You know damn well how hypnotic your pleading dark brown eyes are when you're begging me to share my snacks with you.

And while we're on the subject, I'll never understand how you instantly appear at the table at the precise moment I'm sitting down to eat the breakfast I just prepared. As an experiment, on several recent occasions I've taken great pains to get my breakfast together as quietly as I can, yet you still magically appear exactly when I sit down at the table. My best guess is that with you I'm dealing with a combination of an extremely acute sense of hearing, which you've trained to hone in on the tiniest sounds relating to food preparation, together with a finely tuned sense of ESP with specific regard to food!

Jack: As The Platters used to say back in the '50s, "You'll never know…"

Jack's Dad: On the positive side, Ann and I both love the way you communicate with us by blinking your eyes. Evidently this was originally a silent communication your mom and you both developed to tell each other "I love you," and now I've been included in the loop as well.

Anyhow, I think we're at the point where we need to bring this fascinating discussion to a close.

Jack: I never thought I'd hear you say that – at the beginning I invited you to *start off* sharing some thoughts on the topic, and you ended up hogging almost the entire chapter! Who do you think is the senior author here anyhow?

Jack's Dad: Be that as it may, I'd like to end by sharing some segments of a KMTV interview series with a renowned animal psychic.

Awhile back the British TV program "Animal World: Our Co-Inhabitants" ran a three-part series featuring Sonya Fitzpatrick, a widely respected telepathic animal communicator. Responding to a question concerning the extraordinary loving qualities portrayed by many domestic animals, she related: "All the time you see animals going into nursing homes, and they're helping people...So we feel the love...And they teach people how to love...They're constantly putting out love, and we feel love for them...animals do teach us to love, because that's what the universe wants."

Jack: WOW – That gal sure said a mouthful! Reminds me of the time you and Ann took me down with you to visit your brother who was in the early stages of recovering from a stroke. Your brother and his wife sure didn't want me to leave!

Jack's Dad: Yes, and I remember how patients in the unit were thrilled when you ran into their rooms sporting your little cowboy hat!

Anyhow, I fully agree with Sonja that by far the greatest benefit we humans derive from our interactions with our pets and other animals is that you do, indeed, teach us how to love – provided that we are wise enough to listen and follow your lead. And for that, little buddy, I am eternally grateful.

Jack: Thanks Dad, I'm really touched.

NOTE TO READERS: Hey guys, gals and fellow canines, I'm really excited about the next chapter, which kicks off my five-part sequence on "Training Your Human Parents, Part 1." Stay Tuned!

CHAPTER ELEVEN
Training Your Parents: Part 1 –
Who's in Charge Here?

"Never forget this basic axiom: They think they're in charge, but WE know differently!"

Instructions to Readers: Please note that the following material is for Dogs Only – Violators will be prosecuted to the full extent of the law! Human readers, please turn immediately to Chapter 12. Thank you.

O K fellow canines, I am about to share with you some pearls of wisdom that have been passed down by elite canines since the beginning of time. You, my reader, are now a member of a most privileged class of dogs who have gained access to this wisdom. No need to thank me – Just toss me a good share of your treats!

🐾

So here it is – Jack's Four Basic Precepts for Training Your Parents:

1. Never forget this basic axiom: They think they're in charge, but WE know differently!

   The corollary is: Never, never let them know that you know you're in charge! Indeed, this is where some *very skillful manipulation* on your part is required. With very few exceptions, you must conduct yourself in such a manner that your parents are thoroughly convinced that THEY are in charge! Put yourself in their shoes. As your human parents they like to believe that you are a basically helpless creature totally dependent on them for your wellbeing. As long as they hold that belief, they will naturally be motivated to *care for you* – showering you with affection and, of course, treats!

   Trust me, as long as you adhere to this sound advice you'll be living in the lap of luxury. Disregard this admonition at your own peril. Your human parents must *always* believe they are in charge and that THEY are training YOU. Move on to my second precept and you'll understand why it is so vitally important that you follow my instructions to a tee.

2. At all times remain fully aware of the many perks you will enjoy by virtue of your "allowing" your parents to "train you." Some of the more advantageous of these perks include:

    • Treats!

    • Your parents will smother you with affection when you perform the "tricks" they've taught you at their command.

    • Treats!

    • Their pride in you will swell when they show you off to friends and neighbors – who will probably offer you even more treats!

    • And…did I mention treats?

3. So far I've emphasized the importance of masquerading as a subservient and obedient creature in order to reap the many rewards that will accrue by virtue of employing that posture. However, you must take care to avoid going overboard in playing out this role.

    MOST IMPORTANT – STAND YOUR GROUND when they are teaching you a new trick. More specifically, you must let them know *your ground rules* in no uncertain terms. Namely, "NO TREATS – NO TRICKS"! You must stick to your guns on this one and be unwaveringly persistent – this is especially true as some humans can be very, very stubborn in this regard.

Based on my own experience, I have observed that human moms tend to be more accommodating to your needs here than is often the case with the male of the species. Some dads, in particular, can be very challenging in this regard. All the more reason to STAND YOUR GROUND with them. And, when they finally do come around with the treats, be sure to lavish your affection on them. Remember – positive reinforcement. Surely we all know by now that all members of the human species are suckers for a "cute, loving dog"!

4. Don't be TOO OBEDIENT. Again, this is an admonition to avoid going too far in carrying out the helpless, subservient posture I advocate in conning your parents into believing that they are in charge.

A prime example, every once in a while be sure to "forget" how to perform a particular trick. When that happens they will want to help you "relearn" that trick, and will revert back to food rewards as reinforcement. And guess who benefits in that situation!

Likewise, it's a good idea to include a healthy dose of stubbornness in your interaction with your humans. This will serve to reinforce the subliminal (beneath the level of consciousness) awareness on their part that you are, indeed, in charge. For example, in my case I *never* come when called. (With one exception – FOOD!) While this is totally frustrating to my mom, it keeps her on her toes and makes her aware that I do, indeed, have a strong will of my own!

❧❧

So there you have it, guys and gals, my sage advice in this first installment on "Training Your Parents." Stay tuned for more gems to come in the following chapters.

CHAPTER TWELVE
Keep Them Laughing

"Everyone loves a clown – so ham it up to your heart's content!"

K eeping them laughing is, indeed, one of the key secrets of remaining in good graces with your human family.

As I emphasized in Chapter 8 – Earning Your Keep – Everyone loves a clown – so ham it up to your heart's content! Admittedly I have an advantage here, as I am a clown by nature. I also believe this is one area where we small dogs have a distinct advantage, as we're expected to be cute, cuddly and puppy-like. I mean let's face it, how can any red-blooded, size-challenged dog keep a straight face when confronted with a human mom who's incessantly cooing "Oh, here's my sweet, sweet baby – where's daddy? – where's daddy? – does my baby want to go for a walk?" and other precious gems of doting motherhood taken to an extreme. I must admit, however, that over the course of my evening excursions to the dog park I've seen a number of big dogs do a very credible job of pulling off the clown act.

OK, let's get down to brass tacks. I'll enumerate some of the key advantages that will accrue to you, my fellow canines, through following my admonition to keep them laughing.

1. It's FUN! I'm by far happiest when I'm clowning around, and it's really neat to see my parents pulled into my latest episode of craziness. Children especially (and all humans are really kids at heart) love a dog – or any pet – who constantly keeps them in stitches with their playful antics. That makes YOU an integral and beloved member of the family!

2. Manipulating your way out of trouble – If you're anything like me you're constantly screwing up, like peeing on the rug or whatever. Now when you DO screw up, they'll forgive you much sooner when you immediately tickle their funny bone. My own favorite ploy is to jump up on my mom's lap and stare her in the eyes. After all, who can really stay mad at someone who's making them laugh!

3. Food perks – Keep 'em laughing and they'll give you more treats – and without realizing it they'll probably even increase your meal portions. Hey, you'll have it made, until the next trip to the scale at the vet's office.

4. Whenever one of your humans is feeling down, a heavy dose of crazy humor is by far the best way to pull them out of a blue funk! As a very wise person once said (he must have learned this from his dog) – Laughter is the best medicine!

5. Dispelling boredom – Pulling everyone into your crazy antics is a perfect antidote for boredom. When things start getting slow around my house, I'll grab one of my toys and pull my mom and dad into a game of catch and toss – followed by a royal tug-of-war when I finally retrieve my toy. I'll even leave a toy by my dad's office chair as a hint when I feel he's getting too wrapped up in his work. (Jack's dad – Yes, he really does that!)

OK, I think you've got this one down. So let's move on to another one of my favorite ways of staying in good graces with your human family and, in fact, virtually every other two-legged, clothes-wearing creature you'll encounter.

CHAPTER THIRTEEN
Oh, What a Cute Dog!

*"To be honest, I must admit I'm really quite
the ladies' man."*

As I told you in the last chapter, everyone loves a clown and, I would add, everyone loves a lover.

Cuteness is another area where we small dogs have a distinct advantage due to our small stature and our perpetual puppy-like persona. Think about it – when was the last time you encountered a "cute" pit bull or German shepherd? Getting back to me (after all, that's what this is really all about), when I first entered my new home my mom instantly fell in love with me and my dad immediately followed suit.

Shortly after arriving at my new digs my folks took me on my first visit to the neighborhood pet store. Naturally I was greeted with incessant calls of "Oh, what a cute dog!" as I paraded up and down the aisles. Soon I encountered a precious little 7-8 year-old girl who sat down on the floor with me and treated me to one of the most awesome outpourings of unconditional love I have ever experienced. I tell you, if I hadn't already hooked up with such fantastic human parents I would have seriously considered letting her adopt me right on the spot. (Jack's dad – He conveniently left out that he peed on the wall as soon as he got up from that encounter.)

Back to Jack: To be honest, I must admit I'm really quite the ladies' man. My dad has repeatedly told me that if I put together a charm course for single males of the human species we'd all be rich!

Jack's Mom: Now hold on – I'd heard enough of this little Romeo's braggadocio rambling! Jack, you've embarrassed me on countless occasions when a female passerby would take a liking to you. Remember one of your first walks along the Catalina Nature Trail where a nice woman walking her dog encountered us exclaiming "Oh, what a cute dog!" – and you embarrassed me to tears by immediately growling at her friendly canine companion. At that point all she could do was cry "Oh Dear!" and immediately pull her dogs away from you in disgust. And what about the time over at the doggie park when we were talking with Lu Lu's mom and you attempted to pee on that nice lady's back while she was sitting on the grass?

Jack: Hey – did I ever say I was perfect!

Getting back to my legions of female admirers, I must admit that I am baffled by what appears to be a universal failing on their part. I cannot recall even one incident where these doting members of the fairer sex rewarded me with a treat! C'mon ladies – don't you know that the way to a man's heart is through his stomach?

Jack's dad: Well buddy I wholeheartedly concur with that last statement. My dear wife Ann learned that one at a very early age back in Providence, Rhode Island hanging out with her mother in the kitchen in the early morning hours. Talk about knowing the way to a man's heart via his stomach, she learned that one in spades! The only downside is that whenever we eat out the food always seems second-rate.

Back to Jack: Anyhow, me-thinks we're digressing a bit. Bringing it back to our readers, I'll bet by now you're probably curious about my own encounters with other "cute dogs" that I fondly recall. During our very first morning walk in Riverfront Park (beats me why they call a walking trail smack dab in the middle of the desert Riverfront Park), I fondly recall our encountering a woman with a very cute little poodle-type dog named Sophie, wearing a bow on top her head. I was really warming up to her and SHE had the audacity to rebuff me by growling! On subsequent walks I would admire her from a distance, but she'd always end growling when we got up close. Then I didn't see her for quite a while. Anyhow, next time we encounter Sophie's mom I'll ask my folks to mention that her pride and joy needs a few trips to the doggie park to lighten up and mellow out. Haven't seen either one of them lately. Oh well, as the saying goes – " 'tis better to have loved and lost than to have never loved at all."

Several months after I first drafted this chapter, my dad thought it might be a good idea to revisit it in terms of possible updates.

I emerged out of my mourning over my unrequited love for Sophie several months later when we ran into a very cute and friendly female Chihuahua named Chula. She was accompanied by her mom at Riverfront Park and boy, did we ever hit it off! The clincher came when her mom told us that Chula shares my passion for lizards and *food!* Now there's a gal after my own heart. Unfortunately I've only seen her once after our initial encounter. Man, in today's fast-paced canine single's scene one cannot waste even one second in securing that vital connection during the first meeting. What I'm up against in today's social environment is ever worse than speed-dating at a human singles' club!

Just this morning my folks took me down to Kreigh Park, which houses the Oro Valley Aquatic Center. There we came across a man walking an extremely cute miniature 9-months old female dachshund named Roxie. My mom had a hunch we might hit it off due to my previous co-habitation with a male dachshund at the pound.

WOW – Talk about love at first sight! Roxie and I sniffed, sniffed and sniffed each other, and both my folks and my companion's dad exclaimed that we looked like a match made in heaven. Incidentally, her name is Roxie as her dad explained she has a penchant for eating small rocks. For sure her heart's in the right place, but I've got to teach her a thing or two about hustling real food!

At this point I imagine many readers might be wondering whether I am robbing the cradle, having logged 6 ½ years walking this planet. My response – hey guys and gals, lighten up already! I don't recall any laws concerning the application of statutory rape to canine romantic liaisons. Hey, for all intents and purposes we're two consenting adults, so just leave us alone!

I'm encouraged that both my folks and Roxie's dad seemed to really hit it off. In fact my dad was even telling me I could invite her over sometime to show her my prize collection of toys. As Roxie and her dad arrived the same time we did, my mom made a note that we should make it a point to arrive at the park between 8:10 and 8:20 am. Way to go mom – maybe wedding bells are in yours truly's future after all!

Come to think of it, this recounting of my latest romantic escapade provides a perfect segue to the following chapter "Staking Your Claim in Bed"….

CHAPTER FOURTEEN
Training Your Parents: Part 2 –
Staking Your Claim in Bed

*"Where we end up at bedtime is no small matter,
considering that we spend over one-third of
our lives in bed."*

F or starters, staking our claim in bed is one area where we small dogs have a distinct advantage.

As one who is definitely not a morning person (see next chapter), I fully endorse the adage "Let sleeping dogs lie." But *where* we choose to lie is of utmost importance. I'm appalled that some of my fellow canines accept sleeping on the garage floor or – heaven forbid – in an outdoor doghouse without giving it a second thought. While I believe in different strokes for different folks, a major concession of that magnitude is most definitely not *my* style. Look at it this way – after all the joy and comfort we bring to our human companions, don't you agree we deserve a place of honor in the master bedroom?

Where we end up at bedtime is no small matter, considering the fact that we spend one-third of our lives in bed (in my case, considerably longer). While our self-evident privileged status should ensure us top billing in the realm of sleeping quarters, getting what we want will more often than not require persistent yet delicate negotiation on our part. In essence, we need to be tactfully assertive, effectively asserting our territorial rights while at the same time remaining on guard against coming on too strong too soon.

My advice here – ease your way in. If your parents place your bed-box outside the bedroom, sleep there for a week or so and then begin planting yourself on the bedroom floor just before they bed down. It's imperative to identify which parent is most likely to champion your cause, and work them to the hilt. In my case, I know that my mom is the mother of all bleeding hearts when I look up at her with my big brown pleading eyes. Your mission, should you choose to accept it, is to crank up the charm and the guilt and win that parent over to your side. If this strategy is effectively executed you'll find that in no time at all your bed-box or blanket has been moved into the master bedroom.

Next step, sleep there on the bedroom floor for a week or so – at the same time beginning to hang out with your folks in bed as they read or whatever (well, almost whatever).

The final step – start planting yourself on an unobtrusive spot in bed shortly before they turn in. Remember the eyes – at this point your mom will tell your dad "Oh, it's OK just for this one night." While you may be tempted to cuddle up with your mom in bed - Don't! If you do, you'll quickly learn that husbands can become extremely territorial in their own right. A much wiser long term strategy is to initially sleep in as unobtrusive a spot as possible. *Be patient* – you'll be able to gradually negotiate your territorial prerogative once you've established your claim to a presence in bed.

Once again – ease your way in there and *don't* try to claim too much too soon. Negotiating space in your parents' bed requires that you master and persistently apply the fine art of tactfulness and diplomacy. Disregard this sound advice at your own peril. Do you really want to risk learning the hard way that once you're thrown out of bed, you may end up permanently out in the cold?

For those of you who choose to follow my sage advice in this most delicate area of negotiation - sweet dreams.

CHAPTER FIFTEEN
I'm Really Not a Morning Person

"The joys of sleeping in can never be over-rated."

OK, now that we've established our place of honor in the master bedroom, let's address the topic of high quality, uninterrupted sleep. As I mentioned earlier, this is critically important considering the fact that we spend one-third or more of our lives in bed.

Take it from me, the joys of sleeping in can never be overrated. Sleeping in is one of the many perks of our privileged status as dogs – remember, we're the only creatures on earth that do not have to work for a living. And besides, who's in charge here? YOU of course – and as man's (and woman's) best friend you certainly deserve to fully exercise your royal prerogative of luxuriating in bed while everyone one else is rushing off to work or school.

By the way, this does not in the least contradict my previous advice to permanently endear yourself to your human family by enthusiastically greeting every one of them as they crawl out of bed to start their day. But once you've completed that ritual and – most importantly – had your breakfast, then by all means hightail it back to that warm and cozy bed. My thinking here is driven home by a quote my dad shared with me that is attributed to a *Cat* – of all creatures! Namely, "It's so delicious to spend the morning in bed doing nothing – and then take a nap!"

OK, now I'll describe to you my morning routine. Whoops, wait a minute – my mom is insisting that she write this part in order to "keep me honest." OK mom – let 'er roll!

Jack's Mom: Thanks Jack. That little devil is really a handful when he finally wakes up in the morning. More days than not he wakes up as grouchy as Garfield, and then enthusiastically springs into action greeting us both with slurpy laps on the face and running all over the house with boundless energy, often grabbing one of his toys and initiating a game of catch.

As soon as I'm out of bed he makes a mad dash out to the kitchen, watching intently as I prepare his breakfast (God forbid I should have the audacity to feed myself first). As soon as I set his bowl down he voraciously wolfs it all down in 15 seconds and then – back to bed where he immediately settles into an immovable "Do Not Disturb" posture. If and when he gets out of bed again he hangs out on my lap while I'm reading, or simply lies down on the window shelf beside his couch.

When his dad finally finishes his shower and stretching exercises, I put Jack's harness on – which is his cue to make a mad dash to the garage door. If his dad takes him to the front door for a "quickie" neighborhood walk, Jack ferociously tugs on his leash in the direction of the garage and works on me with his pleading dark brown eyes. I invariably give in and we pile into the car and head out for one of his two favorite nearby walks – Riverfront Park or Catalina State Park. On the way out his dad sits with him in the back seat to calm him down – otherwise he'll don his "macho voice" and bark at every passing walker, car or cyclist – sometimes he even barks at the mountains!

Riverfront Park is his "social walk', where he encounters dogs of all shapes and sizes as their moms fall all over him exclaiming "Oh what a CUTE dog!" This gives him such a swollen head that I never need to worry about his squeezing out of his harness. While he HATES big dogs (as he'll describe in a later chapter), by scratching on his ear and bribing him with treats we're slowly managing to train him to keep his cool.

Catalina Park is our nearby wilderness escape, with miles upon miles of trails going up and down the foothills, featuring awesome panoramic views of the nearby mountains, the Saguaro cacti and a cornucopia of other incredible desert vegetation and wildlife. In this pristine environment our little guy is a hiker par excellence – how can those four little legs ever run so fast? We generally go about 40-45 minutes on the trail, then Jack and I return to a shaded area by the parking lot while his dad continues on for another 10-15 minutes.

Back home he runs into the house like a victorious returning warrior! Then, realizing that he is all tuckered out, he finds a convenient spot (anywhere) to crash and he's out of it for the rest of the morning.

Back to Jack: OK mom – that was really good if I say so myself! And now if you and dad will kindly let me concentrate I'll move on to the next chapter of *my book*. Thank you.

CHAPTER SIXTEEN
A Mother's Love

*"My human mom is the personification of unrelenting
unconditional love. Translation: She spoils me rotten!"*

You know, I'm afraid I was a bit harsh with my mom at the end of the last chapter with my territorial reference to "my book." My dad, a published author, chalks this up to an attack of "author's ego."

Beyond a doubt my human mom is the personification of unrelenting, unconditional love. Translation: She spoils me rotten – and I love every minute of it! What more could any dog in his or her right mind ask for?

My dad claims I start the day as a pampered prince, and I must admit he's right. My mom is generally the first one up, and she starts my day by cuddling, cooing at me and otherwise babying me to the max (another perk of being a small dog). Then she starts her busy day off scurrying around the kitchen, while I luxuriously stretch out on my mattress and savor my remaining time in bed. As you know I most definitely am not a morning person.

There's only one thing that will pull me out of my morning stupor, and you guessed it – BREAKFAST! When my keen ears hear the magical sound of her preparing *my breakfast*, I'm off to the kitchen like a bat out of hell. After breakfast there's no stopping me as I romp throughout the house two or three times at 90 mph. Inevitably I'll pull them into my favorite game – playing catch with one of my toys. While my dad is just dragging himself out of the shower at this point he never seems to mind.

And how that woman showers me with praise. C'mon readers be honest, how many of you receive profuse praise for going to the bathroom (outside of course). My dad, the psychologist, tells me that praise is an indispensable tool in effective behavioral modification. All I can say is that it works with me in spades, especially when combined with a treat, a second treat and yet another treat…

Thanks to my mom, I'm the proud owner of the largest collection of doggie toys in Tucson. When she comes back from shopping I'm right there at the door waiting to inspect her shopping bags for the one containing *my* new toy! This is followed by a mandatory game of catch and tug-of-war, which serves as the rite of initiation for the latest addition to my collection. As I previously mentioned early on I co-opted the living room couch as my day-time pad, which is filled to the max with my growing collection of toys. My mom tells me in all seriousness that she really has to search for me in the midst of all those toys.

And when it comes to food – my passion - my dad swears that my mom is the world's greatest cook. She is half Italian, and my dad has the greatest Paisano's pallet this side of Italy. The only down side, he tells me, is that her culinary arts are such a hard act to follow that eating out is invariably a disappointment. My response – poor baby! While I have to forego the pasta sauce as tomatoes are excluded from my diet, I'm in ecstasy when I get to sample my mom's chicken meatballs!

And did I mention the baths? Once a week she treats me to the most delicious oatmeal bath – a welcome respite from the desert heat. Afterwards I'm in sheer ecstasy as I shake myself dry and romp around the house like a 2-month old puppy.

At this point my dad is warning me that my readers will be curious as to whether my mom is a Jewish mother. So I googled some articles to help me research this topic.

When held up against the traits of a stereotypical Jewish mother, my mom definitely meets the criterion on "endless caretaking and self-sacrifice" – Oy vey – how she worries about me!

However, she fails to measure up to the two essential criteria of "constant overfeeding and urging her children to eat more," and manipulating with guilt. Concerning the constant overfeeding, while I wish with all my heart that applied to her, alas, both my human parents are incurable health nuts who join my vet in incessantly cajoling me to lose weight. And when it comes to the second item, I must confess that *I* am the hands-down expert in mastering the fine art of manipulation by guilt.

To cite a few examples, I superbly excel in begging for table scraps (remember – the eyes have it), although I must admit that my pickings have been somewhat leaner ever since my vet balled out my parents for overfeeding me. However, when it comes to getting my way on the venue for our morning walks, I've honed that one down to a science. When I first joined the family my dad would take me for a morning walk around the neighborhood before embarking on his regular hike. Occasionally the three of us would pile into the car and head out for the awesome trails at Catalina State Park or the more civilized paths at Riverfront Park, frequented by dog-lovers and their pets. Once I got a taste of these outdoor hikes there was no turning back! So whenever my dad puts my leash on to head me out the front door I go right into high gear, tugging like crazy toward the garage door while giving him a defiant stare. Actually he's a pushover as he really loves to hike the trails. So now just about every morning we pile into the car and my mom chauffeurs us off to the wilds. And guess what, everyone's deliriously happy when we arrive at our destination.

My only complaint concerning my blissful home life is my folks' frequently leaving the house without me. I mean, how could they even think about leaving such an affectionate and charming dog behind?

My mom is the biggest offender with her frequent shopping trips. In a state of resignation, I'll sit on the window ledge on the lookout for her eventual return. When she does return I spring into action, racing to the garage door and letting out a series of mournful cries. By the time I get to the door I'm tired of crying and I greet her by enthusiastically jumping up and down on my hind legs.

My dad points out that I'm obviously trying to guilt-trip her as I'll sit there for hours cool as a cucumber until I hear the garage door open. He advises me, "Look Jack, if you're really trying to guilt-trip her you'd better tone up the volume on your cries and keep on crying when she opens up the door." While in terms of sheer logic his advice makes a world of sense, when she finally opens that door I'm so overwhelmed with boundless joy that I can't contain myself! So as much as I hate to admit it, even the world's master guilt-tripper has a chink in his armor when confronted with his mother's love.

And that reminds me, Mothers' Day is right around the corner and I've really got to work on my dad to get on with his arrangements for a beautiful bouquet of flowers and dinner out (I only wish they could take me with them). Stay tuned for the next chapter.

CHAPTER SEVENTEEN
So Now I'm a Marriage Counselor?

*"Getting to know my new parents, I became aware
that my primary role as resident counselor
would be to help them 'lighten up.'"*

Well, so much for Dale Carnegie's myth that a dog is the only creature who doesn't need to work for a living (see chapter 8). Perhaps some of my fellow canines are that fortunate but alas, that is definitely not the case for yours truly. I mean, in my adopted family with a mom who is still in recovery from raising 5 children in a home with only one bathroom, and a dad with a PhD in psychology who is nuttier that a fruitcake, I more than earn my keep functioning 24/7 as a marriage counselor by default.

Before getting into the specifics concerning my own therapeutic orientation, let me first share with you some of the pearls of wisdom I gleaned from my own (ahem) scholarly research. Much of this builds upon insights I provided in Chapter 9 – Is Your Pet a Healer?

An online article by HelpGuide.org titled "The Health Benefits of Dogs (and Cats)" points out that more than any other animal, dogs have evolved (I love that word) to be highly attuned to human behavior and emotions. According to these experts, while we understand many of the words you use, we're even more skillful interpreting your tone of voice, body language and gestures. My dad goes so far as to proclaim that dogs are extremely psychic. Anyhow, the above stated qualifications sound to me like an impressive set of credentials for a highly skilled therapist. So where's my $150 per hour already?

The HelpGuide article goes on to state that dog owners (please – parents, not owners)

- are less likely to suffer from depression than non-owners

- tend to have lower blood pressure, triglyceride and cholesterol levels

- have elevated levels of serotonin and dopamine, which produce a calming effect – and that pet owners over 65 make 30 percent fewer visits to their doctors.

🐾🐾

In addition, research findings demonstrate that heart attack patients with dogs survive longer than those without. More to the point, in terms of therapeutic benefits per se the article reports that "Most dog and cat owners talk to their pets, (and) some even use them to work through their problems," and that a dog's companionship can be extremely helpful in reducing anxiety. More specifically,

"Because dogs live in the moment – they don't worry about what happened yesterday or what might happen tomorrow – they can help you become more mindful and appreciate the joy of the present." WOW – talk about the efficacy of our service as unpaid shrinks – I think I'll raise my fee to $250 per hour!

And finally, researchers have found that through taking their parents on a daily walk, dogs often play a very effective role as "exercise buddies" in helping them lose weight. So c'mon mom and dad, quit nagging me about my own weight already!

Having drawn upon my impressive expertise in laying this informative background, I will now proceed to elaborate on my vital role as an (unpaid) marriage counselor to my adopted parents. I'll begin by asking them to summarize in their own words their state of mind prior to my coming into their lives.

Jack's Dad: I guess I'll go first as between the two of us I've logged by far the most couch time. A bit over 10 years ago Ann and I both retired from our day jobs, sold our home in Southern California and embarked on a major move 1,200 miles up to Washington. In terms of stress overload, this abrupt sequence of major changes left me feeling totally unbalanced and ungrounded.

As I'm sure is the case with many dual career couples, the 24/7 togetherness following retirement brought to the surface a number of relationship issues that had gone unattended while we were both caught up in the fast lane. As I am a rather career-oriented guy who had just published his first book, I was looking forward to launching my new career as a full-time author and speaker who would hopefully emerge as a trail-blazer in my field. At the same time, however, I was becoming painfully aware of the need to take a hard look at my excessive work-related focus, particularly in terms of its impact on the growing emotional distance between Ann and myself. Ann, why don't you take over from here?

Jack's Mom: Yes, our abruptly leaving Southern California where I had spent the greater part of my life and raised 5 children was extremely traumatic for me as well. I missed my family terribly and as time went on we both became disenchanted with our new environment and felt very isolated. We had a lot of clashes stemming from our mutual unhappiness – instead of bringing us closer together as I had hoped would happen, the move to the Northwest drove us further apart. John became overly involved in his writing in a frantic effort to restore a semblance of sanity and predictability to his life, which fed into my own feelings of resentment, loneliness and isolation.

When we moved to Tucson, a sunny desert community and a hiker's paradise, John seemed to thrive in that environment. I still felt isolated and continued to miss my family. While I knew that John was earnestly working on refocusing his priorities and placing our marriage first, we still had clashes. We both needed to lighten up and spend more spontaneous fun time together. When Jack came along it was just what the doctor ordered!

Back to Jack: Hey mom, thanks for the validation – Do I get a treat along with that? Anyhow, it appears that when I entered their home, both my mom and dad were combat-weary from the frequent upheaval they had encountered in their marriage. While they had each evidently done some good individual work with skilled human therapists and were making an earnest effort to work together to restore to their marriage the love and free-flowing, caring communication they had once enjoyed, they were still in a very fragile place in terms of being able to consistently relate to each other in a kind and loving manner.

Jack's Mom and Dad: That about sums it up, Jack.

Back to Jack: Oy Vey – If only the operating manual we dogs are born with contained a detailed chapter dealing with crisis counseling for our human parents! So what was I to do, forced by default into my totally unexpected role as marriage counselor for my troubled parents?

As my dad has told me, any counselor worth his or her salt will inventory the clients' strengths and help them build upon these, while concurrently acknowledging and attempting to shore up the areas of weakness.

From the day we met in the pound, I sensed that both of these people were very much in love. My dad recently shared with me that he had previously been a "cat person," adding that he had opted to go that route out of laziness as he assumed that a dog would require too much maintenance. To his credit, however, he was sensitive to his spouse's longing for a dog. Indeed, he made it a personal mission to work with her to find a dog they would both be happy with, hoping that would help rekindle the joy in their marriage. I probably sensed this at some level when I enthusiastically licked my dad-to-be's beard when we met at the pound. I needed a new home with loving parents, and it was evident that they both needed me.

Getting to know my new parents, I quickly surmised that these were two people who had both been working way too hard and too long in a misguided effort to fill the void between them. I became aware that my primary role as resident counselor would be to help them to *lighten up*, while interjecting heavy doses of much needed play and laughter into their lives. With this knowledge at hand, I resolved to employ the clown side of my persona in interacting with them, both individually and as a couple. Hence I began to start each morning profusely licking my mom in the face while we were still in bed, refusing to stop until she broke into uncontrollable laughter. Likewise, every chance I got I would initiate a game of "catch – tug-of-war" involving one of my toys, knowing that would end with all three of us laughing our heads off!

My dad tells me that through both his training and his own couch time, he has learned that a cardinal rule in any relationship counseling situation is DON'T TAKE SIDES! To be sure, this is most often easier said than done.

One day my mom and dad were sitting together on the couch following a rather difficult verbal exchange. While my natural inclination was to side with my mom, who had succumbed to a rather tearful state, I also knew that *both* of these people still loved each other and that they were both deeply hurting. So what did I do? I spontaneously jumped up on my mom's lap and began licking her face like all get-out. Predictably she couldn't take this very long and shoutcd – "Jack, stop that! You know I can't laugh and cry at thc same time!" Within seconds my mom and dad were both laughing together. Mission accomplished.

While both my parents are avid hikers, my dad used to do most of his daily hikes alone while my mom stayed home or went to the gym. Very soon after I started hanging out with them we developed a morning ritual of piling into the car and heading out for a hike in the mountains or at Riverfront Park. More recently they've started taking me to a doggie park as well.

Do these outings have a positive impact on their relationship? OF COURSE! – they end up filling a good part of each day with lots of hugs and happy quality time together in the great outdoors – and best of all, getting to spend these blissful moments in the company of the erudite and ever-so-charming yours truly!

So there you have it – "Dr. Jack's" crash course in marriage counseling for canines. By the way, if any of you human readers would like to schedule either an individual or a conjoint session with me, my dad tells me you'll be able to reach me via the email address at the end of this book. I'd advise you not to wait too long, however, as I can't guarantee how long I'll be able to hold my fee down to $250 per hour!

CHAPTER EIGHTEEN
Male Bonding

"One of our favorite times together is our morning breakfast (my second, his first)"

L isten up male canines – here's the chapter you've been waiting for!

Despite my sensitive Chihuahua nature I'm really into this male bonding thing. After all, I do have a very masculine side to me. As my dad likes to remind me, after the shelter shaved all the hair off my underbelly, my "member" was so prominent that I would have made a great mascot for Chippendales or centerfold for "Playgirl for Dogs."

As my mom is away a lot during the day with her shopping and other gal-type things, my dad and I spend a lot of time hanging out. I tried to interest him in watching football on the tube with me but that's obviously not his cup of tea. Man, he can't even tell you who's playing in the Super Bowl. He does, however, get real jazzed when Super Bowl Sunday rolls around, as with everyone inside watching the game we have the hiking trails all to ourselves.

Playing cards? You know, I'll bet he'd loose his shirt if I challenged him to a round of poker (I picked that one up growing up in the barrios on Tucson's south side). And sharing a 6-pack – forget it! His specialty as an author is integrating a wellness lifestyle into recovery from alcoholism and other addictions, and he's been a teetotaler for close to 20 years.

What he does excel at is organizing an awesome game of 3-way catch and tug-of-war. He'll grab one of my toys and toss it back and forth with my mom, while they're making the damn thing squeak and otherwise taunting me. Then he'll throw it across the house into the family room and the chase is on! I'll run and fetch the toy and charge all around the house with him chasing after me and bringing up the rear. When I finally get my catch back to my couch the grand finale – the tug-of-war begins! Invariably I'll win and he'll sulk away muttering "Jack, you're just too damn strong!" I often suspect he's letting me win on purpose, but to tell the truth I don't really give a hoot! As a beggar par excellence I've learned you take it when you can get it, and besides we're both having so much fun so who cares!

One of our favorite times together is our morning breakfast (my second, his first) around 11 am in the backyard patio (and I thought I was a late riser). He starts by sharing his oatmeal with me on a small dish (too damn small if you ask me), and I get to lick the bowl when he's finished. Like I said just a minute ago, as a matter of survival we beggars have learned to settle for whatever we can get.

We also hang out when he eats his late night snack. It doesn't matter how sound asleep I am, my ESP alarm system goes off and I'm out of bed like a streak of lightning as soon as he cracks the refrigerator door open. I guess that one of the reasons I like to hang out with this guy is that when it comes to sharing food scraps he's a real soft touch.

And of course we spend a lot of time together in his office working on this book project. Stretching my undersized Chihuahua paws to the keyboard gets rather tedious, however, and I often ask him to take over while I get up and stretch the rest of my body.

Speaking of my dad's office, I really enjoy hanging out there when he does his morning meditation. All I can say is that if you've never experienced the serenity of being with someone in a deep meditation trance you're missing something very special.

So all in all, why do I enjoy hanging out with this guy so much? Well as I mentioned before he's a real soft touch when it comes to sharing table scraps. And come to think of it he's a pretty good pal as well.

🐾🐾

Advice to Male Dogs: Some of you may be thinking "Hey, I'd much rather hang out with my mom. She's the one who feeds me my regular meals, cuddles and babies me and lets me curl up on her warm lap for hours on end." Hey, I gotta admit those are pretty good perks! Just don't entirely ignore the old man, however. Moms also tend to be the disciplinarians, and when you find yourself in the dog-house with her it's mighty reassuring to get a few pats from your dad as a fallback. Also, in many families your dad will be the one who takes you on your walks, so it pays to be on his good side. And what dog in his right mind wants to be booted out of bed by his dad in the middle of the night?

CHAPTER NINETEEN

Training Your Parents: Part 3 — Manipulation by Guilt

John and Ann leaving for dinner without Jack

"By far your strongest ploy in getting your parents to cave in to your demands is manipulation by guilt."

> **Instructions to Readers:** Again, please note that the material in the following two chapters is for Dogs Only. Human readers, please turn immediately to Chapter 21 . Thank you.

L isten up, fellow canines. The basic axiom I posited in Chapter 11 is worth repeating. Namely, your human parents believe they're in charge, but WE know differently! It is critically important, however, that you perpetuate the masquerade that they are in charge. As long as they remain convinced that you are a helpless creature totally dependent on them, they will continue to shower you with affection and will attempt to cater to your every whim. Of course maintaining this façade will require some *very skillful manipulation* on your part.

By far, your strongest ploy in getting your parents to cave in to your demands is – you guessed it – manipulation by guilt! Now wait, don't tune out here on account of all those hackneyed jokes about the stereotypical guilt-provoking Jewish mother. Believe me, those gals are some smart cookies. An astronomical number of them eventually become rich matrons parading down Collins Avenue in Miami Beach, crying all the way to the bank!

So, here is Jack's crash course on mastering the fine, albeit much-maligned art of manipulation by guilt.

Whining is an excellent starting point – and an area where we small dogs hold a distinct advantage. After all, what could possibly appear more pathetic and guilt-provoking that a poor little doggie, head down on the floor, whining at the top of his or her lungs. Believe me, I always turn on the whining act when I hear the garage door opening as my mom returns from one of her frequent shopping trips. Hey, put yourself in her shoes, how could you help but think "Oh dear, I can't bear to see how sad little Jack is after I *abandoned him* for the past hour and a half. How am I ever going to make this up to him?" (HINT: Treats, treats, treats – and don't forget, lunch-time is just around the corner!)

In playing the whining act to full advantage, it's imperative that you wear them down with your persistence. One of my favorite postures is to gaze up at them with my pleading eyes with my head down on the floor, while cautiously beginning to wag my tail. My body language clearly conveys "I'm SO SAD that you abandoned me again and left me all alone. Yet here I am, willing to forgive you." C'mon guys and gals – what mother could possibly resist such an impassioned plea from her little darling. Get this one down and you'll have them eating out of your hand!

Of course my favorite and most successful application of guilt-tripping lies in the realm of begging for food. Man, I've got that down to a science! First of all, from the opposite end of the house I tune in to the most minute kitchen noise and know precisely when my dad is ready to sit down for breakfast. And there I am, tail wagging full speed and my whole body literally bursting with enthusiasm. I'll even dance on my hind legs if that will help! The body language is very clear – "Hey, here I am, your lifelong friend and buddy who is just so delighted to join you for breakfast. Oh, don't mind me – just go ahead and eat while I continue dancing and looking up at you with my big brown eyes." Now tell me, what human parent could resist the temptation to share a generous portion of their oatmeal with me? Not my dad, that's for sure!

Likewise, early on I learned to use guilt to my advantage to take charge and determine where we'll go for our morning walk. On days when they're tired and head for the front door, that's my cue to *immediately* spring into action to short-circuit a short (and boring) neighborhood walk. All this takes on my part is a strong tug on my leash as I re-direct my mom to the garage door, knowing that once we get in that car we're off to a *real hike* in the Catalina Mountains or

Riverfront Park. I can always count on my dad to help me out here, as he hates those "whimpy neighborhood walks" as much as I do.

And of course when both your parents abandon you for an afternoon or evening outing you must immediately pile on the guilt in spades. Bowl them over with those sorrowful eyes – and then wait it out. You'll know they're home when you hear the garage door opening, signaling their return. I've learned from experience that when they've both colluded to abandon me, guilt-tripping them when they return will invariably backfire. So instead I'll apply reverse psychology and roll out the red carpet with boundless enthusiasm the moment they enter the door. I'll run pell-mell throughout the house like a deliriously happy puppy, stand up on my hind legs and hug them both. And before you know it we're engaged in a three-way game of "catch the toy," followed by you guessed it, another round of treats.

Looking at it philosophically, sometimes we just have to accept the inevitable and roll with the punches. And here's the best part – rolling out the carpet when they return enables me to rack up a ton of good karma with both of them, which I'll cash in for food rewards or hold in reserve to soften the blow when I screw up.

Now here's what you need to do when you've messed up royally, such as an "accident" on the carpet or chewing up one of your mom's favorite slippers. I learned this one from my predecessor, Ginger, who appeared one night in a dream. Here's the drill: Nose to the floor accompanied by big-time pleading eyes, which together cry out "Woe is me. I feel so *sorry* and *unworthy* – woe is me!" As Ginger confided, my mom's an all-time sucker for that one – She'll end up feeling guilty for making me feel guilty, which brings a quick ending to my penance "in the doghouse," accompanied by generous food rewards to alleviate her sense of guilt.

OK – Here's a somewhat different twist. If one of your parents steps on you by mistake, or inadvertently lies on you in bed, by all means let out a large "YELP" accompanied by a grotesquely exaggerated look of sadness in your face. This will net you a profound apology, accompanied by an awesome belly-rub or a generous helping of treats – or perhaps both!

One important caveat – NEVER snap back under these circumstances! That is sure to back-fire and could, in the worse case scenario, buy you a one-way ticket back to the pound. If you DO lose it and snap at them there'll be hell to pay. If this becomes a habit, get off your butt and trot down to the nearest anger management class. Believe me, an ounce of prevention here is definitely worth a pound of cure.

So there you have it, "Dr. Jack's" instant crash course in manipulation by guilt. Once again, no need to applaud – just give your food dish a healthy nudge in my direction!

CHAPTER TWENTY
Training Your Parents: Part 4 – When Guilt Doesn't Work

*"Wait until your parents are out of sight
and steal the food you are desperately craving."*

Once again human readers – back off! Thank you.

While generally speaking manipulation by guilt is by far our strongest ploy, I'll be the first to admit that there are times when even guilt won't get you what you want (and richly deserve, in my humble opinion). These situations, while fortunately rare, will require truly desperate measures on your part. I'll cite several examples that illustrate how to successfully con your human parents when even guilt won't work.

Example 1: You're hanging out at the table while your folks are eating, and they refuse to give you any more table scraps, despite your frantically dancing up and down and attempting to hypnotize them with your big sorrowful eyes. Your first recourse, if you haven't already tried this, is to focus your full attention on "working" the parent who is generally the softest touch. Believe me, I can *always* get my dad to give me more food when I tune up my guilt-tripping.

If even that doesn't work, however, then you need to employ a deviously clever tactic that always works for me. The solution: Wait until your parents are out of sight and *steal* the food you are so desperately craving. This works particularly well late in the evening when one of your parents is snacking on the couch, and you've been hanging out with them with your tail wagging non-stop while playing the "big sorrowful eyes" number to the hilt. Often I'll encounter a golden opportunity when my dad is snacking on one of my "forbidden foods," with a small bag of doggie treats by his side. Half the time when he turns in he'll leave the bag of treats on the table by the couch. Now's my opportunity to score *big-time.* As soon as I'm sure he's in bed I'll grab that bag off the table and gleefully scarf down the entire contents. And best of all, when my mom discovers this the next morning she'll take it out on my dad, letting me get off scot-free!

Take it from me, there's big-time rewards to be had if you learn to play the "stealing card" with adroit skill. I've snagged near-full bags of chips off the table on more than one occasion and "inhaled" the full contents quicker than you can bat an eye. And believe me, the inevitable stomach ache is a small price to pay for this scrumptious feast. And finally, if you choose to play the stealing card, just remember that it's *always* easier to gain forgiveness than permission.

<u>Example 2:</u> This one is ideal for puppies who haven't yet mastered the fine art of manipulation by guilt. In this scenario, your folks go out for the evening despite your persistent pleas for them to stay home with you. Now be aware that this ploy I'm about to share with you is not for the weak of heart. Gross as it may sound, leave a pile of brown stuff in the middle of the rug. If you're lucky, when you folks return your mom will feel so sorry that they abandoned their "poor little darling" that she'll insist that your dad clean up the mess, while she refrains from yelling at you. And if you really score on this one, she'll even *reward you* with a generous helping of treats. Who says that crime doesn't pay!

<u>Example 3.</u> You've had a big night and when morning rolls around you are really experiencing the need to sleep in. Meanwhile your folks, anxious to get on with their day, are nagging you to get out of bed for your morning walk. Now on this one you've really got to *put your foot down* and refuse to budge. Go for it to the max – wearing them down with your persistence and showing them who's boss. And if they threaten to go on the walk without you, it's your call. Admittedly this one's a tough call – you've got to weigh and balance how badly you want your morning walk vs. your desire to stay in bed. Regardless as to which alternative you choose, it's of utmost importance that you assume a decisively stubborn stance,

portraying a posture of unmistakable dignity and self-reliance. That way, no matter what you decide they'll know for sure who's the boss!

Example 4: You're on your morning walk and your folks are egging you on to keep moving, as they are obviously tired of your dilly-dallying at every lizard and ground squirrel hole in sight. Of course they are completely missing the point of these morning walks. Again, you must *stubbornly* and persistently stand your ground. If your folks are like mine, you'll eventually wear down their resistance and your dad will break out into uncontrollable laughter at your gung-ho antics as you forge ahead on your mission to chase and catch every lizard and ground squirrel in the park. The one exception: If your folks attempt to bribe you with an offering of treats then by all means acquiesce to their demands. Remember – Food trumps everything!

In summary, if you skillfully apply what you've learned about the fine art of manipulation by guilt, that should get you through 98 percent of the time. In those rare cases where your guilt-tripping fails to yield the desired results, you must then employ every trick in the book to coerce them to cave in to your demands. After all, your commando persona and self-esteem are on the line, and you must employ every means at your disposal to clearly establish who's in charge!

CHAPTER TWENTY-ONE
My Toys

*"Like any well-bred canine I am highly discriminating
in my choice of toys – 'squeaky toys' are definitely in."*

E ver notice how our human parents love showing off their
possessions to their friends, family and anyone else whose
interest they can snag? They'll show off their homes, cars,
children, clothes and even their latest spouse! Believe me, when it

comes to flaunting their symbols of status, anything and everything is fair game.

As American families are very competitively oriented, the question that naturally arises is: "How can I possibly compete with my human parents' ostentatious displays of worldly status?" Don't despair, as through my (ahem) extensive research I've identified two major signs of status we can exploit to the max!

The first lies in the realm of collecting bones. My dad tells me my predecessor Ginger boasted an awesome bone collection that she kept in her special corner of the recreation room. One Christmas eve when everyone was opening and showing off their gifts, she grabbed her new bone and proudly pranced throughout the house waving it for everyone to see. I can just imagine her inviting friends over to admire her bone collection.

While bones are not my thing, I definitely revel in my growing collection of toys. You name it, I've got it – a huge lizard, giraffe, octopus, elephant, rabbit, reindeer, bossy cow and alligator, just to name a few. Like any well-bred canine, I am highly discriminating in my choice of toys. Frisbees, balls and rope toys are out (yawn – boring), and "squeaky toys" are definitely in. When it comes to toys, my motto is "no squeak – no deal!"

Whenever my mom returns from shopping I subject her to a 10-point inspection as she enters the door. Upon greeting her I become overwhelmingly obsessed with one thing and one thing only – "where's my toy?" When I locate the package containing that priceless treasure I'll grab the bag and carry it to my condo (the living room space occupied by the couch and alcove facing out over our front yard). There I proceed to give this latest addition to my stash a thorough going over.

I am admittedly totally possessive of any new toy for the first 24-36 hours. During that time I perform a thorough 36-point inspection. Woe to anyone who attempts to separate me from my latest prize as I meticulously scrutinize it to locate and activate all the various "squeak spots." When I eventually decide to share this treasure with my parents, this momentous occasion becomes big-time cause for celebration as I race through the house flaunting my latest possession. This orgy of self-indulgence finally culminates in allowing my mom and dad to initiate a three-way game of catch ending with a climatic all-out tug-of-war.

As you've probably guessed by now I keep my entire collection in my condo neatly stacked atop the living room couch. Rumor has it that my dad, always the astute businessman, became so disgusted with the prime real estate taken up by my condo that he consulted his accountant regarding a tax write-off based on real property depreciation. Alas, he discovered that was impossible as depreciation is only allowed on bona fide rental property, not a space co-opted by a free-loading pet (source: IRS regulation Schedule E 2014.gwk104073421.screwu2nyrpet).

At this point you're probably wondering whether I ever co-opt any of my parents' stuff for my collection. Short answer – you betcha – anything I can lay my paws on! Some of my favorite pirated toys include my mom's socks and bras (no, I don't have a fetish), assorted slippers and sandals and most recently my dad's watch.

As for my favorite toy, as of this writing the new crocodile wins hands-down. In addition to being highly squeak-able, this coveted possession provides a welcome addition to my total caloric intake. My mom, ever the innovator, stuffs a treat into his mouth and has taught me how to retrieve it. My dad snickers and claims I'm doing CPR on a dumb toy. Do I really give a hoot regarding this derogatory allegation? Hell no – after all I'M the one who's getting the extra treat. Do I detect just a wee bit of jealousy here?

🐾🐾

Note to other dogs: You've probably heard other canines bragging that their toys come to life when their parents leave the house and that everyone parties together way into the wee hours. Is this true, or just another remnant of mythology passed down over the eons? C'mon– do you really think I'd give you the scoop on that one, knowing full well that your snooping parents might read the answer? I'm afraid not – you'll just have to build up your own toy collection and find out for yourself!

CHAPTER TWENTY-TWO
Leave Your Mark on the World

*"Throughout history parents have impressed upon their
offspring the importance of leaving their
mark on the world."*

E arly on in Chapter 6 I described my consuming passion for FOOOOOD! Shortly after settling in with my new parents, however, I began to broaden my horizons as I began to realize that any well-rounded canine worth his salt (why a dog would want to eat salt is beyond me) needs to embrace a *minimum* of three major obsessions that provide the defining focus of his or her life. This chapter and the following are dedicated to expounding on my other two magnificent obsessions.

Throughout history parents have impressed upon their offspring the importance of leaving their mark on the world. When my dad shared this with me it really hit home and I began to ponder "What do I, Jack Newport, need to do to leave my own indistinguishable mark on the world?"

Googling the ASPCA, I came across a post titled "Urine Marking in Dogs." I experienced an epiphany and became aware that marking, otherwise known as "peeing," constitutes the perfect vehicle for leaving my mark on the world. With burgeoning pride I came to the realization that *peeing in style* is, indeed, a highly advanced art form. Now I'm not talking about the mind-set of most canines who give this matter no thought whatsoever and simply pee whenever they have to. Indeed, I'm talking about one's cultivating the skill to elevate what many believe is a relatively mundane function to the state of a truly esteemed art and science. Let me elaborate.

Those truly remarkable members of our species with a bed-rock of self-esteem, who are unequivocally focused on broadcasting their elite status to the world have developed a highly developed art of "over-marking," which consists of reserving a large reservoir of urine to be released on top of the recently deposited urine from a rival canine. Talk about a sure-fire way to establish dominance – Big dogs, eat your hearts out!

Over-marking can also be construed as carefully planning ahead to scatter your urine over all the spots where other dogs have peed first. Believe me, yours truly has honed both of these aspects of over-marking down to a science.

> **Note to female dogs:** Please skip over the following paragraph, which contains invaluable information meant to be shared "only between us boys," so to speak. Thank you.

Now listen up guys – I picked this one up from the ASPCA site. If you really want to score big-time with the ladies you need to be aware that many dogs have learned to skillfully employ the art of peeing in broadcasting their sexual prowess. Pretty cool – huh! In short, "leaving your mark" prominently in all the right places sends a powerful signal to your canine companions of both genders that you are Reproductively Intact. And here's the clincher – to carry it one step further, even if you are neutered you can still broadcast to all eligible members of the species a solid sensation of "reproductive intactness" simply by leaving a healthy dose of pee along the trail in all the right places! After all, as they say in Hollywood it's all about image!

Welcome back ladies, and thank you for allowing me and my buddies to indulge in our locker room chat.

Anyhow, let me share with all of you how I launched my mission of leaving my mark on the world. It all began when my new mom and dad started taking me on morning walks on the Nature Loop at Catalina State Park, a marvelous plateau of exotic desert country that lies several hundred feet above the trail head. I began peeing perhaps 5-6 times along this walk, which is at the high end of the normal range for most dogs. Passing numerous Pit Bulls, German Shepherds and Rottweiler's along the trail, I began to contemplate what I needed to do to make myself truly stand out from the pack.

Eureka! I discovered that by drinking lots of water before leaving home *and* planning ahead as to where to let my bladder loose, I could easily leave a powerful mark on that portion of my world. In no time at all I was peeing 12 – 13 or more times along the Nature Trail, and my dad stopped counting at that point.

Jack's Dad: OK, I've got to interject a note of reality here. Yeah, he *thinks* he's peeing, yet half the time his tank is dry and he doesn't even realize it!

Jack: C'mon guy – let's lighten up! Remember dad, it's all about image, image, image!

Jack's Mom: Now hold on, fella – it's about time I put in my two-cents worth on this one! I mean, I knew that dogs like to pee outdoors and leave their scent to mark their territory. But Jack, I have *never* seen a dog as obsessed as you are with leaving his mark every 30 feet!

Jack, do you have any idea how *embarrassed* I get with your obsessive peeing? It's getting to the point where I'm afraid to take you anywhere. I mean, I can't take you to the pet store without your peeing on a pole. And the height of embarrassment is when we take you to the dog park. Rather than socializing with the other dogs, you are totally focused on scoping out all the spots to pee on – you even end up peeing on the other dogs without even realizing it!

Jack: Hey, did I ever say I was perfect?

🐾

Anyhow, I guess it's time to move on to my other recently discovered obsession. Stay tuned for the next chapter!

CHAPTER TWENTY-THREE
Lizards for Breakfast

"Piggy-backing on Arizona Governor Jan Brewer's Blockbuster book 'Scorpions for Breakfast' I'm planning a sequel to this book titled 'Lizards for Breakfast'."

When my dad is not helping me with this book, he spends a lot of his time keeping on top of the local political scene. He recently shared with me that former Arizona Governor Jan Brewer, who is not exactly known for her calming demeanor, made a fortune off her book "Scorpions for Breakfast." Being a shrewd promoter, she boosted her book to best seller status through a photo-op that captured her angrily waving her finger as she greeted President Obama on the runway deplaning at the Phoenix airport.

Piggy-backing on her idea, I'm planning a sequel to this book titled "Lizards for Breakfast." I'm even planning my photo-ops for the book's launch. In the highly unlikely event that my forthcoming presidential campaign fails to produce a land-slide victory (see Chapter 31), a prominent shot of my peeing on the newly-elected President's leg will clearly land my sequel in the New York Times best seller list! The following is a sneak preview of this forthcoming blockbuster book.

My folks and I agree that a key perk of living in Southern Arizona is the abundance of desert flora and wildlife practically at your doorstep. From the window of my condo facing the street I am greeted each morning by a cute little bunny that scarfs down the scraps of broccoli my folks leave out for him. About that same time my serenity is invaded by a big-ole pesky lizard that occupies the same exact spot on our sidewalk every morning, prior to planting himself right beneath my window to taunt me.

Our back yard attracts a menagerie of wild birds, including an occasional predatory hawk. The latter's sudden unexpected appearance is a key reason why my parents refuse to let me roam the back yard, which is great lizard hunting country, without a leash. We've also spotted coyotes and owls in the wash directly below our yard and have witnessed several sightings of road runners and their favorite meal, lizards. Early one morning my folks even saw a huge bobcat on a patio right outside our family room. Evidently he was attracted by drippings from a sprinkler that had watered our plants just before sunrise.

In the immediately preceding chapter I described my obsession with "leaving my mark on the world" during our morning walks. Several months ago, when we shifted our daily walks from Catalina State Park to the shadier Riverfront Park to escape the summer heat, I felt like a kid in a candy store and became a first-class lizard hunter in no time flat! By the way, my dad tells me Tucson has two seasons – summer and January – which is when they break out the long-sleeved Hawaiian shirts.

Anyhow, my mom's been peeking over my shoulder and is edging me away from the keyboard, so I'll let her relate to you my "Lizards for Breakfast" saga in her own words.

Jack's Mom: Well, it's about time I manage to get a word in edge-wise on this opus you two have been cranking out over the past several months.

One thing I will say about Jack – that dog is *different!* I described his unbelievable obsession with urination in the preceding chapter. Then when the spring months came around and we retreated to Riverfront Park to escape the heat, that guy developed a whole new obsession – lizards and ground squirrels!

It started innocently enough one morning as we were rounding the path at the far end of the park and he spotted a ground squirrel peeking out of his hole at the other side of the fence. We let Jack crawl under the fence and approach his new-found friend, and they had a royal game of hide and seek going for the next 20 minutes. There were two squirrels in that hole and they enticed him to wait for them to reemerge at the top of the hole. Meanwhile they would crawl through the tunnel to another hole and surprise Jack by coming up behind him.

For the next several weeks Jack insisted on daily stalking the hole where he had found the squirrels. After the first day the squirrels decided they'd had their fun with him and had better things to do.

Fortunately for Jack he discovered his new grand passion – lizard hunting. While you won't spot any lizards during a cloud cover, as soon as the clouds clear they come out from their holes to bask in the sun. There's one half of the trail that we call lizard country, and our little guy is as familiar with every nook and cranny as he is with the underside of his paw.

When we approach the lizard territory Jack takes off like a bat out of hell and there's no stopping him. As I hold on tight to his leash he gives me a workout to end all workouts – I must have shed at least 10 pounds on that trail thanks to his frantic lizard hunts! As we near the end of the three-quarter mile loop we enter chuckwalla territory and all hell breaks loose. While the chuckwallas high-tail it to the top of the wall where Jack can't reach them, he couldn't care less as he's totally caught up in the frenzy of the chase.

You're probably wondering if he ever actually caught a lizard or ground squirrel. Not on my watch. However with his dad, who's obsessed with protecting him from developing an inferiority complex, it's a whole different story. One morning at the edge of the lizard territory Jack spotted a baby ground squirrel. His dad, who was walking him at the time, actually encouraged him to wait for the squirrel to reemerge from his hole. He even let him catch the squirrel, although I scolded them both and made Jack let him go unharmed.

Another time Jack was walking with his dad in the opposite direction from the spot where he had sighted the baby ground squirrel. This time he encountered a medium-sized horned toad which his dad let him catch. Again, I chided them both and made Jack release the little critter, much to his chagrin.

Jack's Dad: OK, I admit I feel sorry for him when he never catches a lizard, and I want to make sure he has some successes to reinforce his delicate ego.

Jack's Mom: What delicate ego?

Jack's Dad: OK, I guess I was being just a bit facetious. I do agree with you, however, on the importance of making sure he releases his catch. Kinda reminds me of the approach that some fishermen take to fishing for sport – enjoy the fun of the catch and toss the fish right back in the water.

Jack: OK, are you guys finished for now? I'm anxious to move on to the next chapter. And dear reader, be prepared for more exciting escapades ahead and be sure to be on the lookout for my sequel to this book – "Lizards for Breakfast." All you need to do is keep checking the New York Time's best seller list.

CHAPTER TWENTY-FOUR
Big Dogs (and why I hate them)

*"What we small guys lack in size we more
than make up for in sheer brainpower."*

Why do I hate big dogs? In a word, because they're BIG!
Put yourself in my shoes – How do you think I feel
constantly encountering these monstrosities with over-
active pituitaries in the parks and on the trail – especially after
practicing my deep-throated growl over the past 5 ½ years? It just
isn't fair – period!

Beats me why any human in their right mind would even think of having a big dog in the first place. For one thing, I've seen big dogs as huge as small horses and believe me, they'll eat you out of house and home at no time at all. Even worse, they'll monopolize your couch space and crowd you out of bed (husbands beware!). And let's get serious, who would really want to travel with a big dog in tow? They'll take up far too much room in your car, resulting in decreased gas mileage. And taking one on vacation – forget it! While many modestly priced and even upscale hotels will accommodate *small* pets, at times for a nominal surcharge, with a big dog your lodging options are basically limited to staying with relatives (yuk!), camping or settling for a one-star motel. Not my idea of a really fun vacation. I could go on and on, but I think you're catching my drift.

By contrast, let's consider the unique virtues endemic to the smaller members of our species. At the outset I submit that we smaller dogs make far superior pet material for reasons far too numerous to cite in this book. For starters, we are cute and cuddly, we fit perfectly on your lap, and many of us maintain a charmingly playful puppy-like personality throughout our entire lives. Let's face it – everyone loves a puppy or a kitten, but do you really want to share your home with a grouchy, set-in-his ways Labrador or an obstinate and ornery Tom-Cat?

Likewise, the smaller members of our species are much easier on the wallet – especially when it comes to feeding, and we leave behind far less poop to pick up. Whoops - My dad is calling me a hypocrite in touting the benefits of lower food consumption. Oh well, maybe I'm just the exception that proves the rule.

And readers, having read this far into my opus, I'm sure that you'll agree that the smaller members of our species are by far endowed with a superior intellect. It all goes back to Darwin, I guess. What we small guys may lack in terms of size we more than make up for in sheer brainpower.

But you know what really gets my dander? When we encounter a couple on the trail with a big dog and I begin growling at this *intruder,* that dog's humans will knowingly smile at my parents and say "aha, he's got a Napoleon complex!" From my perspective, they've got it *all wrong* here – if anything, Napoleon suffered from a small-dog complex. For one thing, as he was The Napoleon, how could he possibly harbor a "Napoleon complex"? I'll betcha anything he was the runt of the litter growing up in Corsica, France.

Now Russian President Vladimir Putin is a whole different story. Historically traveling in the footsteps of Napoleon Bonaparte he may indeed suffer from a Napoleon complex, although I personally suspect he more appropriately falls into the small-dog complex classification. Estimates of his height vary from 5'2" to 5'5", and Kremlin insiders report that strict rules dictate that no members of his entourage can be taller than the president. I know the guy prides himself on his athletic prowess, and I truly believe that his over-aggressive international posture represents a compensation for his short stature.

He also has an obsession with super-models and his long-time girlfriend, 32-year old Alina Kabaeva is a knock-out standing 5 ft 5" as well as a gold medal Olympic gymnast. You know, that couple could really learn some tricks from yours truly. I'll bet that if his girlfriend scratched him behind his ears he'd calm down in no time flat. I should really write the Department of State about this. I've even thought of volunteering to serve as an ambassador to Russia, except that having spent my entire life in the desert I'm a warm weather person, and my dad warns me that Moscow can get *mighty cold.*

As the saying goes, good things come in small packages. A word to my compatriots – small dogs rule!

CHAPTER TWENTY-FIVE
Stand Your Ground

*"I unequivocally assert my exclusive right
to all new toys and watermelon rinds."*

> **Warning:** This chapter is for *small dogs only*. Human violators will be prosecuted to the full extent of the law and *big dogs* – don't even think about venturing into this territory. As even I have my moments of kindness toward the larger members of my species, big dogs who violate this warning will get off with a strict written warning on the first offense. Repeated violators, however, will be swiftly escorted to the paddy wagon for a one-way trip to the pound.

Now that I've made myself clear on the ground rules, small dog readers listen up! As you are well aware, we more petite members of the canine species (I like to refer to us as the "petite elites") must exercise constant vigilance in both attaining and maintaining our rightful status in a world dominated by both four-legged and two-legged creatures who are eager to lord it over us by virtue of their sheer size. The good news is that in this chapter I will share with you time-honored wisdom passed down through the ages, secrets that are guaranteed to make others look up to you at all times, even though they think that you are "small." For those of you who are up to the challenge – read on.

First let's address head on the issue of putting all those big dogs in their proper place. For starters, you need to assume a warrior mode and master the fine art of GROWLING by practicing every chance you get. For example, when my mom and dad are driving me out to Riverfront Park or Catalina where I know I'll most likely encounter a good share of larger dogs on the trail, I psych myself up by standing up in my elevated doggie seat and barking big-time at everything in sight. You name it – other cars, runners, cyclists, women pushing baby carriages – anything and everything is fair game! Remember that when you're riding in a car, especially a SUV, you are high above both the traffic and pedestrians. WOW – talk about a perfect launching-pad for a power trip! GO FOR IT –

hold your head up high with your tail wagging like a metronome and let 'er rip – barking at the top of your lungs to your heart's content!

After a few minutes of psyching yourself up in this manner and getting the adrenalin surging though your system, by the time you get to the park you'll feel ready to take on ANYTHING that crosses your path – mountain lions, grizzly bears and, of course, those pathetic over-sized dogs. Note of Reality: Even though you *feel* ready to tear into all those huge creators, as they say in the stunt-driving commercials "Don't try this at home." Rather, employ the tactics I'll describe in the following paragraph to broadcast loud and clear to those big dogs *and* their humans the message "DON'T MESS WITH ME!", *while at the same time* remaining safely ensconced in your parent's protection.

When you encounter a big dog (on a leash of course) on the trail, if he wants to come close to check you out, play nice for a second or two and then GROWL! Take it from me, the shock value alone will put you in a whole different league with that big guy and his human – like "Hey, let's back off – this guy is *serious!*"

Now comes the icing on the cake – *each and every time* you encounter a big dog on the trail, as described in the preceding chapter your mission is to unequivocally broadcast *your territorial ownership* by prominently leaving your scent – i.e. peeing – on all key spots throughout the turf. The message you leave speaks loud and clear to every passer-by – "I was here."

Ready for more on standing your ground? OK, here's a bit of a refresher course. As I previously emphasized in my initial chapter on "Training Your Parents," even though your underlying objective is to get them to follow your lead by manipulatively perpetuating the delusion that they are in charge, there are times in even that arena where you must clearly stand your ground.

Of utmost importance, when they are teaching you a new trick you must firmly and unequivocally enforce *your rule* of "NO

TREATS – NO TRICKS!" For crying out loud, why even think of giving them a freebie when you have a golden opportunity to walk away with a belly full of treats? Unquestionably maintaining the illusion of subservient obedience will reaps huge rewards on many occasions. There are, however, times when you must depart from this precept in order to assert your independence and reinforce your parents' subliminal realization that *you* are, indeed, in charge. For example, I *never* come when called, and at times I'll be totally obstinate just to "mess with their heads."

Question: Do you passively let your parents take you on a walk of their choosing, or do you call the shots? As you've probably guessed, I've staunchly opted for the latter from day 1.

Sometimes (out of sheer laziness I'm sure) my parents will put my harness on and head for the front door, which to me signifies "Yawn – another boring neighborhood walk." My immediate response is "No way Jose!" Knowing I need to step forward im-mediately to stand my ground, I dash out to the garage door wagging my tail while tuning up the volume on my excitement. If my mom already has the leash on me so much the better – I'll just drag her along with me. All of this triggers a dialog between my folks concerning where we should go. Now's the time to pour on the *guilt trip* big-time – accentuated by the guilt-provoking eyes, whining and whatever else it takes. And you know what, I can't recall the last time I failed to get my way on that one!

It is also essential to effectively assert our territorial prerogative on holding our own in regard to special possessions. I unequivocally assert my *exclusive right of possession* in regard to (a) new toys and (b) watermelon rinds. While I normally coax my parents to play a 3-way game of "catch the toy" followed by a tug-of-war which I invariably win, when I'm breaking in a new toy it's *hands off* to all two-legged and four-legged creatures – no ifs, ands or buts! While this is one of the very few times I recommend growling at your parents, in this case it's an absolute territorial imperative. *Warning: Don't ever get carried away and end up snapping at your parents, or any other humans for that matter!* No matter how understanding you think they may be, you'll be *most unpleasantly surprised* to learn how quickly they may scoop you up and whisk you back to the pound on that one. Indeed, discretion is the better part of valor.

As I write this we're at the peak of the summer heat and I've recently developed a mega-obsession with watermelon rinds. Don't ask me why, I just find those morsels intoxicatingly delicious. Standing my ground with my watermelon rind securely positioned in my mouth, my vocalizations and body language broadcast the message "BACK OFF!!" in no uncertain terms. I'm afraid this one might have back-fired, however, as yesterday I overheard my mom tell my dad "No more watermelon rinds for you-know-who!"

As an afterword to chapter 14 – Staking Your Claim in Bed – once you've managed to ease your way up to that juncture, occasions may arise that dictate the need to stand your ground in that particular arena. As my mom and I generally sack out half-an-hour before my dad, from time to time I'll plant myself lying full length across the bed a bit below my dad's pillow. Don't ask me why – I guess I just enjoy "messing with his head" when he finally decides to turn in.

As you can see, while my calculated moves to stand my ground may occasionally back-fire, all-in-all I have to admit I've got a damn good batting average! In closing, fellow members of the "petite elites," just follow the (ahem) sage advice I've imparted throughout this chapter and you'll be sitting pretty big-time!

CHAPTER TWENTY-SIX
On the Road

"I've heard that travel is broadening, but my folks are already nagging me about my expanding back-side."

WOW – If there's anyone with an aversion to traveling, yours truly definitely fits that category. Sure, they say that travel is adventurous, but aside from my daily walks and other local outings I'm basically a home-body. Let's face it, I've got a "great deal" here and I LOVE my home. I mean I've got my own condo complete with a breath-taking view of the Catalina Mountains, two well-trained parents, great hiking and lizard hunting country practically at my door step, and an abundance of FOOD. Have I got a great deal or what! I've also heard that travel is broadening, which I probably don't need as my folks are already nagging me about my expanding back-side.

As it is, however, my mom has a large family back in California, so like it or not I'm becoming a seasoned canine traveler – kicking and screaming all the way!

Before my first trip to California my parents took me on a trial run half-way to Phoenix. This turned out to be a total disaster – between my throwing up and my folks getting lost, that was not exactly our finest hour.

I wish my dad would accompany us on all our road trips, but he tells me he's not all that crazy about returning to Southern California. I've really got to hand it to my mom, however, she's got the whole ordeal of juggling road trips and dog-sitting down to a science. She makes sure we leave super-early to minimize our exposure to the heat and we generally arrive at our destination by early afternoon.

Undoubtedly the worst part of being on the road is the M-word – Motels. While we have stayed in some really great motels, some of the places that accommodate dogs and other pets are the tackiest dives I've ever seen! I mean c'mon already – what self-respecting canine wants to sleep surrounded by the overwhelming aroma of other dogs' pee on the carpet? (Yes, we definitely have an acute sense of smell.)

I've been tempted to apply for a gig as a consultant to a so-called pet-friendly hotel chain – except that I'd have to spend most of my time on the road imparting my wisdom to the hotel managers and house-keeping staff. No way Jose – I'm perfectly happy snuggling up with my parents in my own bed in my own home.

I am, however, looking forward to our upcoming trip to San Diego this summer. The promise of dog-friendly beaches, parks and walking trails does indeed sound enticing. Watch out all you female Chihuahuas sunning yourselves on the beach at Mission Bay – "Beach Boy Jack" is heading your way – YAHOO!

So what do I enjoy about these travels with my mom and dad? I suppose a real benefit is the opportunity to bond with my extended human family. The constant accolades of "Oh, what a cute dog!" are music to my sagging ego as I attempt to recover from a day-long drive across the desert.

On a recent trip to LA we attended a reception for my Aunt Barbara's son Alfred, who had just graduated from the University of Central Florida. I'm told that the bill of fare at the elegant restaurant was sumptuous. Due to a cruel twist of fate, however, I was confined to the car during the entire feast. Once again, where is the ASPCA when I really need them?

For sure one of the highlights of these trips is visiting with my human parents' granddaughter Amber – such a cute and loving young lady. I'd take her home with me in a heartbeat if only they'd let me. (Editor's Note: Several months after Jack drafted this chapter Amber did indeed move in for an extended stay with her grandparents and Jack.) During that same trip my mom and dad took me to the awesome beach at Corona Del Mar, and I also got to join everyone for breakfast at a wonderful sidewalk café in Orange.

On our last trip to California, which my mom and I made alone, I spent several nights at my uncle David's house, sharing the turf with

Ruby, their pet "pug." This was a first for me, and despite our mutual trepidation I must admit that all in all we got along rather amicably.

By far the best part of these road trips is coming home at last. We usually arrive back home in the evening, when it is pleasantly cool. For hours on end during our drive back to Tucson I dream of entering the door, running through the house non-stop and engaging my exhausted parents in an endless round of "catch the toy"! Indeed, home is where the heart is, along with my soft bed, my treats, the food, my toys – and did I mention my treats? Indeed, I am in sheer ecstasy when we finally arrive back home.

CHAPTER TWENTY-SEVEN
A Trip from Hell,
with Slices of Heaven

"By far the greatest slice of heaven on this trip was my day-long visit with my latest girlfriend, Gigi."

S peaking of travel, I just got back from a hellacious trip to California. We left late in June and returned the early part of July. My mom, organized as ever, got us loaded into her SUV with all our stuff at the crack of dawn and we hit the road at 5:30 am. Despite her superb planning, however, it was HOT traveling 500 miles across the desert. As we are both adverse to hanging out at the rest stops along the freeway, it was essentially a grueling non-stop trip with the exception of a few very brief pit stops. And to add insult to injury, on the way back we even had trouble with the air conditioner. Oy vey!

When we finally arrived at my aunt Shirley's in North Hollywood I let out a huge sigh of relief. Thank God, I thought, now I can finally kick back and relax. As luck would have it, however, Murphy's Law prevailed. First of all on the streets and sidewalks of LA, as is probably the case with all major cities, the tension in the air is so thick you can cut it with a knife. So there went my morning walks – I mean, am I going to willingly subject myself to all that mega-stress? No way!

As anyone who has visited LA is painfully aware, Southern California epitomizes the worst possible manifestation of urban sprawl, which introduced into our daily lives a constant back and forth over super-crowded freeways as we visited the far-flung members of my mom's clan. (As my dad constantly reminds me, there's no such thing as a small Italian family.)

As it cooled off a bit in the evenings, I assumed that I could finally relax and ease my frazzled nerves. No such luck – we were clearly in the midst of a battlefield of major proportion surrounded by gunshots each and every night. And believe it or not, the banditos actually followed us home and our oasis of serenity in Oro Valley was surrounded by gunshots our first night back home! My dad must have chased them away, however, as we heard no more gunshots from that point forward.

Jack's Dad: I need to interject a note of reality here. Jack and his mom arrived in North Hollywood on the first day of the week before the Fourth of July, and the locals went gung ho with their stockpiles of fireworks every night until well past midnight. And Ann, to her credit, drove them back on Monday, the Fourth of July holiday to avoid the normal weekday traffic jams. So as fate would have it, Jack's first night back home was the Fourth of July, where our own locals went bananas with their firework stashes.

🐾

Back to Jack: OK, now that we've gotten the bad stuff out of the way, I'll take the rest of this chapter to highlight those aspects of our trip that were truly memorable.

By far the greatest of these was my day long visit with my latest girlfriend Gigi, who lives with my cousin Chuck's friend next door. Her mom brought her over to visit Chuck and she ended up spending the lion's share of the day with me. My aunt told my dad she's a Maltese, and hands down she's the cutest little canine gal I've ever laid eyes on.

I was so infatuated with Gigi that when we got back home I did a google search on the Maltese breed. A slide show on Animal Planet was most informative – here's what I learned. Did you know that Maltese are the richest dogs in the world? According to Animal Planet, a Maltese named "Miss Trouble" inherited a $12 million fortune! Hey Miss Trouble, I've got a solid reputation as a trouble maker myself – me thinks you and I could make beautiful music together. Hint If you ever need any help spending that $12 million fortune just give me a call! You can either reach me at my dad's number or track me down via my implanted chip.

Getting back to what I learned, the Maltese are evidently the epitome of canine glamour – they were even the pets of choice for both Marie Antoinette and Elizabeth Taylor! These canine beauties are long-haired and most definitely are not cheap dates when it comes to grooming. Aside from their long hair, other distinguishing features are their dark round eyes and cute button nose. While they are predisposed to a great temperament they are not particularly recommended for families with small children. Hmm, could there be a bit of sibling rivalry at play here?

Getting back to my day with Gigi, while she's a bit on the shy side, we got in lots of licks and hugs throughout the day. To be sure, we were both heart-broken when her mom finally brought her back home. It really warmed my heart when my mom talked with Chuck shortly after we arrived back home, and relayed to me that Gigi's been combing every inch of my aunt's house searching for yours truly.

My mom tells me that aunty Shirley and aunt Barbara might be driving out to see us sometime in September or October. Hey mom – hint, hint – why don't they bring Gigi out here with them? I'd sure love to spend days on end showing that little cutie around the Old Pueblo. Well until then, at least I can dream…

🐾

Next on my hit parade for this trip was our day-long trip up the coast to Ventura Harbor. Man, do I ever love prancing up and down the beach, breathing the fresh salt air and chasing the sea-gulls *and* other dogs along their dog-friendly beach! Unfortunately, despite numerous reminders from my dad before leaving home I forgot my surf board.

And of course there were all the delicious servings of FOOD – served by folks who (thank God) do not share my folks' penchant for curbing my caloric consumption. I'm talking about the truly fantastic meals served by my mom and her two sisters, together with our scrumptious meals at various exotic outdoor cafes. Talk about slices of heaven!

And the grand finale, just before we headed back home, was our visit with my human grandson Liam in Santa Ana. Liam is my mom's first great grandchild and I can't begin to tell you how much I just *love* that little baby. Did I say little? Man, at just 6 ½ months that guy is already bigger than me! A note to my folks – hint, hint – I don't see his parents, David Jr. and Carmen, constantly goading Liam concerning his voracious appetite. I could go on and on concerning how much I love that little guy and look out for him – which will be the topic of my next chapter.

CHAPTER TWENTY-EIGHT
My Human Grandson

*"If his folks need any help with potty training
I'll be happy to take him to the park and
show him my favorite peeing spots."*

lthough I'm a confirmed bachelor, I have a strong paternal instinct when it comes to looking out for puppies, human babies and other young creatures smaller than myself. By the way I'm sure you're familiar with the classic definition of a bachelor: A man who has no children to speak of. On our daily walks very young small dogs, especially females, appear to be especially attracted to me. No doubt this reflects my gallant knight in shining armor persona I portray to the women of the world, without regard to species.

Anyhow, during my last trip to California we spent an afternoon visiting my human cousin David and his wife Carmen, together with their newly arrived first child, Liam. This was the first time I remember seeing a human puppy (sorry, baby) up close, and that little guy really made a lasting impression with me. His parents tell us he weighed 8 ½ pounds at birth, and he is already bigger than me. As my human cousin David is the proud father, I guess that makes me his canine grand-dad. And man I'll tell you, I couldn't be prouder!

At 6 ½ months Liam already has a captivating smile, that little guy is really going to be a charmer. And should he ever desire any coaching in that area, yours truly will be eagerly standing by to help out. I was spellbound when my mom held him in her arms, and just sat there staring up at him with my big brown eyes. I can't wait to take him walking with us a bit down the road, and train him how to catch lizards and ground squirrels. And if his folks need any help with potty training I'll be happy to take him to the park and introduce him to my favorite peeing spots. Always ready to lend a helping hand – that's me!

I sometimes wonder if I was a sheep dog in a former life. I definitely seem to have an instinct for guarding the herd. A bit later we adjourned to the dining room to sit down for supper. By the way I always enjoy dining with folks I just met, as they invariably think it is "so, so cute" when I jump up and beg for table scraps. Why my human parents get so jaded with my begging is beyond me.

Anyhow, when we big people sat down at the table I was constantly on the alert concerning Liam's welfare. If I heard him stirring I'd immediately turn my head in his direction. And whenever he would cry I would immediately run to his side to calm him down. If that didn't work I'd run back to my mom, looking up at her like a "worried mother." Jack's Mom: That is most definitely true. I'll tell you, if anyone in our family is a "Jewish mother" it's him, not me.

Back to Jack: Anyhow, being intrigued by my own paternal instinct regarding my human grandson and similar qualities I had observed in other canines, when we got back home I decided to do some on line research on the fascinating topic of humans who were allegedly raised by other species. If you enjoy watching movies from a former era you are no doubt familiar with the saga of Tarzan, king of the jungle, who was allegedly abandoned as a child and raised by apes.

Googling "humans raised by animals," I came across a number of recountings of humans being raised by canines, including our cousin the wolf. According to legend Romulus and Remus, twin brothers who founded the city of Rome, were abandoned as children and were suckled by a wolf until they were discovered by a wandering shepherd.

Other accounts include Oxana, a Ukranian girl who was left to live in a kennel by her abusive parents from ages 3 to 8. When discovered by authorities, she was unable to speak, choosing to bark, and ran around on all fours. Likewise, a girl named Madina was recently discovered who lived with dogs until age 3. When found she only knew two words, yes and no, while preferring to growl like a dog.

Accounts of "feral children" raised by wolves include a story involving a mysterious girl seen running on all fours, attacking a herd of goats near San Felipe, Mexico in 1845. She was reportedly again sighted in 1852, suckling two wolf cubs on a sand bar in a river. And in 1920 two girls, 8 years and 18 months old, were found in a wolves' den in Midnapore, India. Because of their difference in age it was presumed they were not sisters but were taken in by wolves on separate occasions. A most unusual account involves John, the Ungandan monkey boy, who fled to the jungle at age 4 after seeing his mother murdered by his father. He was reportedly raised by a troop of vervet monkeys until his discovery in 1991. During that time his adoptive monkey family assisted him in resisting his capture by humans. His human adoptive family eventually taught him to speak and sing, and he reportedly went on tour for several years with the Pearl of Africa children's choir.

Closer to home, my dad tells me that his youngest brother, Jerry, learned to talk from a pet crow wandering around their back yard.

Jack's dad: Yes, that's right. I was about 8 or 9 and had a pet crow, Blackie, whom I retrieved from his nest when he was very young. Our field guide instructed me to teach him how to talk by gently stuffing small pieces of bread and milk down his throat each morning, saying "hello" whenever I did this. Sure enough, as he grew older Blackie learned to talk and he loved to walk around our back yard yelling "hello" at the top of his lungs. He often yelled this incantation walking by my baby brother Jerry's window, and sure enough Jerry's first spoken word was "hello"! Interestingly, my grown brother Jerry and his wife Mary are fascinated by birds, and housed a large menagerie until they recently downsized their living quarters.

Back to Jack: As you can see, there are many examples of animals raising small children abandoned at an early age, with many of these involving members of our canine family. Both my dad and I are fascinated by these striking examples of grown animal nurturing small children and welcoming them as equal members into their own families. Putting on his psychologist hat, my dad ponders the possible existence of a profound nurturing instinct that often transcends differences in species when an abandoned human child or other young creature is discovered.

CHAPTER TWENTY-NINE
There's a New Sheriff in Town

"Strolling down the sidewalks of downtown Sedona, AZ I encountered a really mean looking dude with his pistol pointed directly at me!"

R ecently I joined my folks as they drove up to Sedona to celebrate their 30th anniversary.

On the way up we stopped at Prescott, AZ, a gun-toting

replica of the wild west which also boasts the cleanest air in the country. Walking the downtown sidewalks I was leading the charge and naturally led my folks into a pet store, hoping to hustle some treats while they roamed the aisles. In keeping with our sojourn back to the Wild West, my folks bought me a snazzy cowboy hat, dark brown with an awesome black band bearing a REAL LIFE SHERIFF'S STAR!

As you can see from my head shot at the beginning of this chapter, my new regalia immediately announced to all passers-by that there was, indeed, a new sheriff in town! You should have seen me strolling up and down the streets of Prescott, chafing at the bit to tangle with the first big dog that dared to get out of line. As all good things must come to an end, however, after a leisurely lunch in the town plaza we headed back to the car and off to Sedona.

Arriving in Sedona, we checked into the Arrabella Hotel, which got its name from Mrs. Sedona Arrabella Schenebly, after whom the town was named. As my dad constantly reminds everyone, one of his best friends back in Tucson is former KGUN TV anchor Larry Schnebly, a direct descendant of Sedona's founding couple. That evening during dinner at a pleasant outdoor café we witnessed the tail end of a lunar eclipse and then headed back to our room.

The next day we began our grand tour of beautiful Sedona, surrounded by awesome red rock boulders, plateaus and mountains – My dad claims that Sedona is truly one of the seven wonders of the world.

Strolling down the sidewalks of downtown Sedona, I encountered a really mean looking dude, an hombre with his pistol pulled and pointing directly at me. At last – an opportunity to cement my status as the new sheriff in town! I stood up tall and proud on my hind legs and began a barking marathon that lasted the next several minutes. My encounter with this bandito attracted quite a crowd – throngs of human onlookers who, marveling at my bravery, were vociferously cheering me on! With that mean old hombre cowering before me, the crowd gave me a rousing round of applause – At that moment I knew that I had truly arrived as the new sheriff in town on the sun-drenched streets of Sedona.

Jack's Parents: Hold on fella, don't you think you're going just a wee bit overboard here? Yes, we did encounter a "mean old hombre" on our stroll through town, but you conveniently forgot to mention that this figure was actually a life-size cardboard caricature of one of the bad-men who walked the streets of Sedona in the mid-1800s.

And yes you did, indeed, attract quite a crowd of on-lookers. However you neglect to mention that they were laughing their heads off at this head-strong little dog barking his head off at this cardboard replica!

Jack: Details, details. As Hillary Clinton would say, it's all over so what does it really matter at this point?

🐾

Okay, you guys have had your fun. Let me remind you that we have a submission timeline to adhere to, so I'd suggest we can the frivolity, get back to work and move on to the next chapter. Thank you.

CHAPTER THIRTY
Training Your Parents: Part 5 –
Keep Them on Their Toes

"Keep your parents constantly frustrated by refusing to come when you are called."

ONCE AGAIN – NO HUMAN READERS ALLOWED!
Please skip immediately to Chapter 31 – The Grand Finale.
Thank you.

O K fellow canines – In a nutshell the theme of this lesson is: The best way to ensure that you remain in charge is to *constantly* keep your human parents a bit off center. That way they'll never be quite sure what to expect from you – and the uncertainty will drive them bonkers! Below is a sampling of my favorite tactics for keeping my folks on their toes:

1. As I've admonished you before, keep your parents constantly frustrated by refusing to come when called. However, it's wise to make an occasional exception to this general rule. On those rare occasions when you DO come when called, your folks will be racking their brains wondering what's going on with you. Psychologists call this tactic "intermittent reinforcement," and it will absolutely drive your parents up the wall – What fun!

2. If you're anything like me, you will *always* be raring to go on your morning walk. Just to keep things interesting, occasionally pretend to be sluggish and totally disinterested when your mom announces it's time for your walk. That will play on her sympathy big-time, and you'll be rewarded by an outpouring of extra attention ("What's the matter, poor baby? Did we get you out of bed too early?")

    And especially at that time of day, she's bound to favor you with some additional treats to help "poor baby" get out of being down in the dumps.

3. Even though by now you should be well house-broken, spice up the routine by leaving a bit of hardened poo-poo on the carpet in the middle of the night. Be sure to do this only on

very rare occasions. If your mom is anything like mine, when she discovers this the next morning she'll immediately assume the burden of guilt ("Oh dear, we should've taken him out right before we went to bed") – and all is forgiven.

By now you may be asking, "Why should I go through all this trouble just to get my mom off center?" OK, here's the scoop - What I'm advising you to do here is a classic example of conditioning your parents to leave you alone when you really do mess up. What you are really doing is slowly yet persistently conditioning your parents to immediately *forgive you* when you really do screw up! TWO IMPORTANT NOTES: Remember I've advising you to leave just a tad of *hard* doo-doo on the carpet. The soft kind is a real pain to clean up and will most assuredly get you in the dog-house!

Likewise, NEVER intentionally pee on the carpet as a ploy for keeping them on their toes. That will most assuredly backfire and in addition to having your nose rubbed into your own pee you'll find yourself in some very deep doo-doo, to say the least.

4. In earlier chapters I've advised you to bark your head off at everything in sight while you're being driven to and from your morning walks. Modifying this routine – Get your folks off center by occasionally remaining still on these rides and not making a sound. Your mom will profusely praise you, while your abrupt change in behavior will drive your dad nuts!

5. This is a great one to pull when you're lying around the house feeling bored. *Disappear* to someplace where it's impossible to find you – be sure to do this at least every other day. Think of all the fun you'll have witnessing your mom go through hysterics trying to find her "poor little baby," while your dad is laughing his head off! Actually, my dad shared with me

that their former cat, Mystery, honed this one down to perfection and even carried it one step further. While his mom was frantically running about the house trying to find him, all of a sudden he'd reappear in a very prominent location, with his body language signaling that he'd been there forever. Gotta hand it to that cat!

🐾

So there you have it, Jack's primer on how to secure your base of power while constantly keeping your human parents on their toes. Read on – the best is yet to come!

CHAPTER THIRTY-ONE
Grand Finale – Vote for Jack in 2020!

"The country's going to the dogs –
Let's make it official!"

Well, we're getting close to the end of my opus and I must say that writing this book has really broadened my horizons and boosted my self-confidence. In fact, as the 2016 presidential election approached I gave serious thought to tossing my collar into the ring and running for President! In terms of strategy, however, I decided to sit that one out and concentrate on building a solid base of support to capture the White House in 2020.

And why not? Heck, over the months leading up to the 2016 election my dad and I discussed our nation's dismal state of affairs on numerous occasions. I distinctly recall his always ending these dialogs with "One thing's for sure, Jack, in the upcoming presidential election it would really be difficult to do much worse than what we've had to put up with over the past 15 years!" I agreed wholeheartedly, our country was definitely in need of a change.

Of course in my process of making my monumental decision to run in 2020 I first needed to address the core issue – Am I eligible to run? Having thoroughly researched that item, I can confidently state that all signs are pointing to an affirmative answer. Let me briefly enumerate some key factors:

1. I clearly meet the qualification that a President must be native born. I was definitely born and raised in the good old USA, even though rumor has it I started out my life in the southern tip of Arizona, not far from the Mexican border.

2. A President must be age 35 or older to serve in office. Again no problem. By the summer of 2020 I will have logged a bit over 10 ½ human years on this planet, which equates to 74 dog years. Assuming that reasonable accommodation will prevail in the interest of assuring a fair and level playing field for all candidates, I foresee no problem whatsoever in meeting that criteria. And lest you think my campaign will be a repeat of Bob Dole's run, I come from an extremely long lived species with an average life span of 17 years, which

equates to 119 dog years. Heck, relatively speaking I'll be just a pup!

3. Recent historical precedent – Now that one's the clincher. Referring back to a scandal up in Washington State that made the headlines back in 2016, if a white woman can serve as president of the Spokane, WA chapter of the NAACP, I see no reason why a full-blooded canine should not be able to run for President. Everyone says the country is going to the dogs, which I contend makes me the perfect candidate.

And speaking of precedent, my exhaustive research reveals beyond a doubt that there are countless incidents of dogs becoming actively involved in American politics at both the local and national levels. More to the point, a recent computer search turned up numerous cases in which politicians and their adversaries have emulated our exemplary canine behavior in the day-to-day battles that are part and parcel of our political landscape. The following examples are just the tip of the iceberg:

- Headline in *Tampa Bay Times*, February 10, 2015. "Hillsborough School Board *dogged* by politics, perception as superintendent search begins."

- *USA Today,* August 23, 2005. "Bush *dogged* on vacation by critics."

- *Los Angeles Times*, October 24, 1993. "NEWS ANALYSIS: Clinton *Dogged* by Failure to Clarify Foreign Policy."

- *New York Times*, October 17, 1989. "Washington at Work; Beset by Critics Hungry for Dynamic Leader, *Dogged* Mitchell Lashes Back."

Wow – that last headline is the clincher as it emphatically depicts both the Senate majority leader and his critics going overboard in emulating our canine behavior!

In all fairness, I should make it clear that blatant examples of public officials bending over backwards to emulate our canine behavior are by no means limited to the United States. Case in point: a March 26, 2015 post on the British SunNation blog titled "12 Politicians That Look Like Dogs" presents a dozen photos of British pols doing their very best to pose as look-alikes to yours truly and my fellow canines.

And finally, an undated post titled "McCain dog" (google online) contains a collage of photos showing Arizona Senator John McCain posing as a dog, including a hilarious shot of him imitating a dog while sticking out his tongue, together with poses of him growling and posing as a bull-dog. Hey, come to think of it, that guy has a field office right here in Tucson. I should drop by and pick his brain regarding my campaign!

An Interview with Candidate Jack

I am fully aware, of course, that any aspiring candidate worth his or her salt must become adept in the art and science of campaigning, including handling debates, media interviews, stump speeches, kissing babies (lick, lick), playing the rubber chicken circuit (yum, yum), etc. With that in mind I've asked my dad to conduct a candidate interview with me as a trial run. He suggested that we focus on how I stack up against Donald Trump and Hillary Clinton, who fought a contentious battle for the White House in 2016.

Jack's Dad: OK Mr. Possible Candidate Jack, assuming that you run where will you align yourself in terms of party affiliation?

A: That's a very interesting question, one that I've carefully pondered over the past several months. Originally I was leaning toward running as a Republican candidate as their campaign cycle starts early on, which I believe gives their nominee an edge in terms of public exposure.

Looking back on the recent election, what swayed me was a discussion we had back then where you stated that if current trends continued, by the time the summer of 2016 rolled around the number of GOP candidates would outnumber the pool of prospective voters. Worst case scenario would point to a similar trend as 2020 approaches. Being wary of that prospect, I've decided to run as an Independent. Interestingly, in my home state of Arizona the population of registered voters breaks down into approximately 1/3 Republicans, 1/3 Democrats and 1/3 Independents.

Q: Again, assuming that you run what will your platform be?

A: Platform? I'm surprised that you raise that question after all the hikes we've taken together in the desert. As depicted below my platform will be the top of my favorite boulder in Catalina State Park, where I can see miles ahead in any direction.

Candidate Jack's Platform

Q: Well that wasn't exactly the response I was expecting. Getting down to practicalities, let's suppose that Hillary Clinton wins the Democratic nomination in 2020. As you know, women constitute the majority of adults in this country, and during the 2016 election many pundits firmly believed she had the women's voting bloc sewn up. Strategically, how would you propose to counter that formidable opposition?

A: That's really quite simple. Referring back to Chapter 13 "Oh What a Cute Dog!", if I say so myself I'm really quite the ladies' man. You can't tell me that you haven't noticed how the gals just swarm around me practically everywhere we go. You just wait and see, by the time my campaign kicks into gear I'll have the nation's women literally eating out of my hand! Of course, when they offer me treats on the campaign trail then I'll be eating out of their hands. But the fact remains, I'm fully confident that given my indomitable charm I'll clearly have that key segment of the electorate in the palm of my hand.

Q: Where do you stand in regard to voting rights?

A: I unequivocally believe that every adult American should be fully supported in exercising their right to vote. In fact, once I am sworn in as President one of my top priorities will be expanding voting rights to encompass a sizable segment of our population that has been disenfranchised for far too long.

To be more specific – Were you aware that the *U.S. Pet Ownership and Demographics Sourcebook* estimates that there are 69,926,000 dogs in the United States? That breaks down to 36.5 percent of all households with one or more resident canines, with an average of 1.6 dogs per household. (Hmmm, wonder if my size qualifies me as a whole dog or a 1/3 dog?) With everyone claiming the country is going to the dogs, it's imperative that this potentially vital voting bloc become immediately empowered.

Q: Getting back to the competition. We all know that Donald Trump defied all predictions and garnered a majority of the 2016 electoral vote. Assuming he's still in office, he will be the incumbent in 2020. What are your strategic thoughts concerning how you would attempt to beat him out?

A: You know, that's one heck of a good question (that's the standard response from pols when they don't have a ready answer.) I gotta admit, that guy showed a lot of moxie in the 2016 campaign. His meteoric rise to the top was, to my knowledge, unprecedented and the fact that he was largely able to finance his own campaign was a definite plus with many voters. And let's not forget that one strong advantage that we share is that we are both perceived as political outsiders.

Assuming he will be the incumbent in 2020, however, I will need to carefully consider my strategic options. As of this writing he has definitely had a roller coaster ride concerning his ratings in the polls, and is having an incredibly difficult time forging consensus within his own party. Indeed his popularity with voters has plummeted to an all-time low. If these difficulties continue to plague him throughout his term I would definitely view myself as a worthy opponent.

On the other hand, if by some miracle he manages to effectively collaborate with both houses and both sides of the aisle and is able to deliver on some signature promises, I would definitely need to reconsider my strategy. At that point I would read his book "The Art of the Deal" and seriously consider approaching him about our joining forces on the same ticket. Under these circumstances I would seriously consider the Vice Presidential spot, provided that he were willing to concede to two non-negotiable points. These are: (1) he must guarantee me a lifetime supply of high quality treats, and (2) he must promise to strongly champion my proposal to extend voting rights to all native-born American dogs, culminating in a Constitutional Amendment by the end of his tenure.

Q: OK, let's address a different topic. Many presidents, including our current president and his immediate predecessor, have been criticized for assuming an aloof and condescending posture in regard to the legislative branch of government. If you are elected, how do you intend to maintain a meaningful level of interaction with members of both houses of Congress?

A: First of all, I promise to maintain a high profile by visiting both the House and Senate on a weekly basis. Upon my arrival I'll enthusiastically dash up and down the aisles before assuming my (ahem) rightful position at the podium. In addition, I firmly intend to get to know each member of Congress on a personal basis. For starters, I'll approach each member and sniff their butt. If they reciprocate then I'll know they're someone I can trust. For those who refuse to reciprocate – sorry guys and gals, all deals are off!

Q: Now let's turn to the international arena. As President and Commander-in-Chief, how do you propose to defend our country against the very real threat of terrorism?

A: That's simple. The realm of international negotiations is definitely an area where we small dogs have a decided advantage. I'll reach out to both our allies and adversaries and win them over with my cute and cuddly charm. If that doesn't work, I'll stand up tall and fiercely bark at them until they come around. And as a last resort, I'll sic my 70 million fellow American canines on them! Hell's bells – with me in charge we'll have our enemies cowering while concurrently achieving massive savings in military expenditures associated with troop deployment.

Q: OK, let's cut to the chase – What do you believe you have learned that will enable you to demonstrate to voters that you are Presidential material?

A: I firmly believe that the hallmark of an effective leader is the ability to portray an effective balance and blending between appropriately exercising his or her authority, tempered by judicious self-restraint. As my human parents will readily attest, I effectively exercise my authority in all situations via my predisposition to be a manipulator par excellence. I have also acquired considerable wisdom over my 40+ dog years pertaining to the realm of self-restraint. Early on, I learned that one must refrain from peeing on the carpet, even when one feels their bladder is about to burst. I have also learned that it is inappropriate to pee in a pet store and in other shopping areas that humans tend to frequent. And finally, in the course of my evening outings with my parents I have learned it is definitely not in good form to pee on the back of a woman sitting on the grass at the dog park. Now if that's not presidential material, I'll eat my hat!

Q: That's a relatively safe statement, as I notice you are wearing a dog-collar rather than a hat. Now, returning to our current president's predecessor – What is your opinion concerning his frequent complaints that "They treat me like a dog!"

A: First of all, I'm a dog and am proud to be a member of the illustrious canine species. So what's so bad about being treated like a dog?

I would add that the operative term here is the word "TREAT." What the heck, if my colleagues in Washington and even the lobbyists are willing to throw a generous amount of *treats* my way, I'll be more than happy to bend over backwards to give them whatever they want!

Interviewer: Well, so much for stamping out corruption in politics.

🐾

So there you have it readers, my first interview on the campaign trail. Admittedly there are a few bugs to iron out. Anyhow, as the 2020 election year approaches, be on the lookout to see me on the campaign trail at a corner near you. And don't forget to bring your treats!

Jack's Parting Words

In closing ladies, gentleman, boys, girls and last but not least, fellow canines, I feel extremely privileged to have had this opportunity to share my seasoned reflections on the world around me. WOW – think about it, I'm one of the first bona fide authors to bridge the gap between two distinct species. As my dad would say – not too shabby!

I hope that in some small way I have inspired my human readers to embrace a fuller appreciation of the myriad members of the animal kingdom that cross your path each and every day. I also hope you will feel motivated to form a deeper bonding with whatever pets frequent your abode, be they royal members of the canine family, a bird, a goldfish – or even a lowly cat. I believe with all my heart that we domesticated creatures were put on this planet to bring a special presence of love, joy and comfort to you, our human companions. We're all in this together – so let's make the most of the wonderful journey we were intended to share together as we follow our paths across this rich green earth.

In peace,

Jack

AFTERWORD
Our Four-Legged Guardian Angel

Hi, this is Jack's dad again.

Upon reflection it's predictable that I would wind up with an animal as my alter ego. My path in that direction began with the inspiration of two wonderful people who both came into my life a bit over 30 years ago. The first is my loving wife Ann, who continues to teach me the true meaning of love and devotion, and introduced me to the wonders of becoming immersed in nature through hiking in the wilderness. The second is my good friend and mentor, Dr. Steven Farmer, who inspired me to follow my calling as a writer and also encouraged me to open my spirit to the innate wisdom inherent in our natural surroundings through engaging in the time-honored Native American tradition of communing with animal spirits. I invite you to read either of Steven's books on this fascinating subject, *Animal Spirit Guides* and *Pocket Guide to Spirit Animals.*

After moving to the desert six years ago I have become increasingly attuned to the spirits of the animals, birds and reptiles I encounter in my morning hikes along the trails. I am no longer surprised by the totally unexpected and sudden appearance of an animal or bird whose spirit communicates to me precisely what I need to learn at that moment. My animal guides have included Road Runner, Hummingbird, Wolf, Coyote, Raccoon, Jack Rabbit – and now Chihuahua.

Space does not permit me to fully describe how much love, warmth and sheer joy our little Jack has brought to our lives. He's brought Ann and me immensely closer together through our morning walks, our ritualistic three-way games of "catch the toy" and fondly shared reflections concerning his latest antics.

Our house literally comes alive with his boundless energy and contagious exuberance over the sheer joy of being alive! He immediately senses when we are going out without him. Although he is obviously saddened he automatically lies down and patiently waits for us to come back. When we return we are given the royal red-carpet treatment – accentuated by his dashing all over the house and immediately initiating a 3-way round of "catch the toy"!

In short, that little guy is perfect for us. We never cease to be enthralled by the well-spring of enthusiasm that springs from his perpetual puppy-like nature. He is extremely perceptive and attuned to both of us, especially in terms of bringing us up when we are down. He truly has an uncanny sense of knowing when either of us is feeling tense or sad – and responds by instantly jumping up on our lap, wagging his tail non-stop and covering our faces with doggie-kisses.

And does this guy ever want to be a part of our family! When we are sharing an embrace he immediately runs over, jumps up on his hind legs and looks up into our eyes, clearly wanting to be a part of that very precious moment.

These are just a few of the very special surprises we are constantly blessed with through Jack's presence in our lives. Hey, I could go on and on. Simply put, this little guy continues to bring so many awe-filled moments into our lives – moments that bring us closer to each other and to this marvelous little creature who miraculously came into our lives. Yes, beyond a doubt little Jack is truly our four-legged guardian angel.

About the Authors and Photography Staff

Jack "K-9" Newport, Senior Author

Jack is a seven year old, 8-12 pound Chihuahua – Jack Russell mix. (His weight varies with our diligence in monitoring his diet.) He is a native of Tucson, Arizona, which he claims qualifies him as a bond fide American citizen. His hobbies include food, hiking in the desert with his human parents, food, chasing lizards and ground squirrels, watching movies on TV and…did we mention food? While this is his first book, he swears it definitely won't be his last!

John Newport, Senior Assistant Author and Business Manager

John has previously published four books, including "The Wellness-Recovery Connection" (Health Communications, Inc.) and "The Tucson Tragedy: Lessons from the Senseless Shooting of Gabrielle Giffords." He has a PhD in psychology and according to Jack is "nuttier than a fruitcake." In addition to being a wannabe jazz vocalist, he and his wife Ann share a passion for hiking in the beautiful Sonoran desert.

Ann Newport, Assistant Author, Photographer and Copy Editor

Ann hails from Providence, Rhode Island and is by far the better half of this five-some (we never claimed to be mathematicians). She credits her finely-honed organizational skills to having raised five children in a house with one bathroom. She is the heart of her family (if you don't believe me just ask Jack) and her hobbies include creative Italian and multi-cultural cooking, photography, playing the piano and hiking in the desert and along the seashore.

Amber Luanne Hollinger, Director of Photography

Amber recently moved from Southern California to Tucson and is currently living with her grandparents Ann and John and, of course, Jack. She is a highly skilled abstract artist (website: www.etsy.com/shop/amberluanneart), photographer and computer whiz, and is completing her studies in Landscape Design at the University of Arizona. Upon moving in with Ann, John and Jack she was immediately drafted to

serve as Director of Photography for this project. A wise choice indeed!

Adam Ditt, Photographic Design Specialist

Adam is Amber's significant other who currently lives in Southern California. His passion is playing bass guitar and he currently plays with a Costa Mesa based band "Professor Colombo." In addition to his talents as a musician, Adam also shares Amber's passion for art and is a highly skilled on-line graphic designer. He has made an awesome contribution to this project through creating amalgamations of straight photos and orchestrating other special effects.

Authors' Website

For further information about *"The World According to Jack,"* including a blog giving updates on Jack's latest escapades, his presidential campaign, upcoming events and more visit our website www.jacksworldk9.com.

Coming Attractions

Between now and November, 2020 we anticipate offering Jack's fans a variety of opportunities to actively support his presidential election! Among other things we are considering a "Vote for Jack" kit featuring a bumper sticker and campaign buttons. You may want to bookmark our website www.jacksworldk9.com and periodically check in for updates. Also be sure to check for possible book signings and other events in your area. (Jack's fully prepared with his paw stamp.)

Contact Us:

Jack would love to hear from his readers (besides eating, sleeping and chasing lizards he really doesn't have that much to do). He invites you to contact him or his Senior Assistant Author and Business Manager Dr. John Newport at our project email address healingtucson@hotmail.com. (While Jack does have an imbedded computerized chip, he prefers to be contacted through his business manager and special assistant John Newport.)

Invite Us to Do a Road Show

Jack and his Senior Assistant Author "Dr. John" are available to come to your chosen venue to do a presentation at a conference, another large meeting or a TV presentation. For further information contact Dr. Newport at healingtucson@hotmail.com.

Information for Media:

We would love to hear from media representatives seeking the "inside scoop" on Jack and his unique perspective on the world around him. We welcome requests for Radio/TV interviews and/or feature articles for both print and online media. Our co-author and business manager John Newport is a frequent guest on several talk shows in Arizona and Los Angeles. Visit our Press Kit on Jack's website www.jacksworldk9.com.

Partnership Opportunities

We are seeking prospective partners for "win-win" collaboration in concurrently promoting your business or organization and our book. We have a number of creative and **FUN** opportunities available we would love to discuss with you! To initiate a dialog email us at our project address healingtucson@hotmail.com.